"There is something unsettlingly, incande⟨⟩...ly specific about the portrait of the Blake family in Stephen Karam's funny, poignant, even chilling new comedy-drama, *The Humans* . . . The playwright delves into the dynamics of this clan with a gentleness that feels like compassion and a scrupulousness that borders on the forensic . . . *The Humans* is the sort of impeccably constructed play that should be a regular inhabitant on Broadway, not the occasional, surprising guest."

—PETER MARKS, WASHINGTON POST

"Karam, whose flair for character and context was evident in the 2012 Pulitzer Prize finalist *Sons of the Prophet,* isn't interested in a polemic. *The Humans* rather considers the trials its highly imperfect subjects face in a highly imperfect world, and resolves, without ever approaching sentimentality, that love is nonetheless resilient."

—ELYSA GARDNER, USA TODAY

"A play of uncommon strengths; fresh, funny, piercing and perceptive. *The Humans* isn't just a family portrait—it's a mirror. Karam has an eye for detail on a near cellular level, an ear for authentic dialogue and a superlative ability to balance laughter and sorrow."

—JOE DZIEMIANOWICZ, NEW YORK DAILY NEWS

"*The Humans* is an absolute triumph."

—MARK KENNEDY, ASSOCIATED PRESS

"The formula for a family-reunion play goes like this: Multiple generations of a clan get together for a holiday, air their dirty laundry at dinner, start fighting over dessert and at the end of the day are weary of battle. Stephen Karam's warm-hearted play *The Humans* follows the formula, but only to the point of exposing everybody's secrets. Instead of erupting in bitter hatred, Karam's characters respond to these revelations with deep love."

—MARILYN STASIO, VARIETY

"There is so much love, dread, tenderness and brutality in *The Humans* that it is hard to believe just ninety minutes pass through Stephen Karam's deeply felt family tragicomedy thriller . . . *The Humans* burrows into the lives of an Irish-American family with wit, tenderness and blistering brutality."

—LINDA WINER, *NEWSDAY*

"A quietly stunning new play by Stephen Karam . . . The beat-by-beat honesty, wit and intelligence of the writing kept me alert to every changing nuance. It has completely earned its place on the Broadway stage; and does so without the supposed benefit of star casting. What will sell it is the play itself."

—MARK SHENTON, *STAGE*

"There's no plate-smashing moment that you see in more histrionic family-gathering dramas (all the flatware in Brigid's apartment is plastic anyway). Each of the Blakes, even Momo, are masking major tragedies in their lives, but even those are revealed in ways that feel utterly unforced. Some moments are absolutely devastating—but it's unfair to label the play as simply "depressing," because it's depressing in the way life is depressing and hilarious in the way life is hilarious . . . Karam's transcendently mundane play is a reminder that family dinner dramas can still be surprising—and they don't need ghosts or things that go bump in the night to achieve that. Real life is scary enough."

—STEPHAN LEE, *ENTERTAINMENT WEEKLY*

"*The Humans* is a funny, mournful, richly detailed and deeply humane study of a beleaguered family celebrating Thanksgiving dinner in a tumbledown Chinatown apartment."

—ALEXIS SOLOSKI, *GUARDIAN*

"*The Humans* is monumentally affecting, and something for which theatergoers should be oh so very thankful . . . An eloquent and wholly relatable modern family drama. I loved *The Humans*."

—ROBERT KAHN, NBC

"We feel a tidal wave of emotion at *The Humans* . . . Never has there been a more realistic encapsulation of the electricity generated when multiple generations come together under one roof."

—ZACHARY STEWART, *THEATERMANIA*

"Stephen Karam's beautiful, funny-sad and ultimately wrenching portrait of a troubled lower-middle-class Pennsylvania family . . . builds on the ample promise of Karam's earlier works, confirming him as a uniquely probing investigator of the contemporary American psyche."

—DAVID ROONEY, *HOLLYWOOD REPORTER*

"*The Humans* is tremendously exciting theater. Karam's fine sophomore play *Sons of the Prophet* was a Pulitzer finalist; *The Humans* takes him to an even higher level. You won't see a better play this year."

—JEREMY GERARD, *DEADLINE*

"Though this is Karam's first Broadway transfer, it shares with his previous plays a knack for unlocking our darkest, coldest truths through precise application of light and heat. This bestows upon what is, at least at first, a pretty typical dysfunctional-family drama new layers of depth, weight and significance that make this as effective and affecting as anything the Main Stem has seen in years."

—MATTHEW MURRAY, *TALKIN' BROADWAY*

THE
HUMANS

———

THE
HUMANS

_____

Stephen Karam

Foreword by Samuel G. Freedman

REVISED EDITION

THEATRE COMMUNICATIONS GROUP
NEW YORK
2016

The Humans is published by Theatre Communications Group, Inc., 520 Eighth Avenue, 24th Floor, New York, NY 10018-4156

Epigraphs: *Think and Grow Rich* by Napoleon Hill was first published by the Ralston Society in 1937; Penguin, New York, 2005. *The Uncanny* by Sigmund Freud was first published in *Imago*, Bd. V., 1919; *The Uncanny*, Penguin, New York, 2003. "Dance of Death" by Federico García Lorca, published in *Poet in New York*, Grove Press, New York, 2008.

The publication of *The Humans* by Stephen Karam, through TCG's Book Program, is made possible in part by the New York State Council on the Arts with the support of Governor Andrew Cuomo and the New York State Legislature.

TCG books are exclusively distributed to the book trade by Consortium Book Sales and Distribution.

LIBRARY OF CONGRESS CATALOGING-IN-PUBLICATION DATA
Karam, Stephen.
The humans / Stephen Karam.
pages ; cm
ISBN 978-1-55936-542-0 (softcover)
ISBN 978-1-55936-863-6 (ebook)
1. Families—New York—Drama. 2. Interpersonal relations—Drama.
3. Domestic drama. I. Title.
PS3611.A72H86   2015
812'.6—dc23   2015032787

Book design and composition by Lisa Govan
Cover design by Mark Melnick
Cover photographs: Jonathan Knowles/Getty Images (statue);
Carlos Casariego/Getty Images (New York skyline)

First Edition, October 2015
Revised Edition, April 2016
Second Printing, June 2016

FOREWORD

By Samuel G. Freedman

Midway through Stephen Karam's masterful play *The Humans*, several generations of the Blake family sit down to Thanksgiving dinner. They sip wine and chug beer as the table fills with platters of food, and they pass the final moments before the meal chatting about a popular zombie show on TV. "Yeah, well," the mother and matriarch, Deirdre, cuts in to say, "there's enough going on in the real world to give me the creeps, I don't need any more."

That passing comment, uttered within a few seconds, could serve as an epigraph for the entire play. For what Karam began writing as a kind of homage to stage thrillers like *Wait Until Dark* evolved over time into the sort of ghost story in which the phantoms are all too real. The darkness that frightens and finally envelops his characters comes literally from an event as prosaic as light bulbs burning out. Those faltering lights, in turn, stand for the social forces that leave the Blakes clinging ever more precariously to the middle-class life that is supposed to be an American birthright.

One definition of great art might be that it knows the news before the news has even happened. Indeed, as it opened Off-Broadway in late 2015 and transferred onto Broadway early the following year, *The Humans* indelibly captured a mood of national anxiety about income inequality and economic stagnation that animated the divisive and polarizing presidential campaign in 2016. Yet, as much as *The Humans* distills a contemporary moment, it is a work informed by decades of history, history as lived by Karam and his forebears.

Karam was born in 1979 in Scranton, Pennsylvania, once the commercial hub of a coal-mining region. On his paternal side, Karam descends from Lebanese immigrants, specifically a grandfather who raised ten children on a tailor's wages. The maternal line is Irish Catholic, with a grandfather who was a newspaper typesetter besotted with the words he assembled in lead. In a Scranton that was still thriving, each family achieved its upward mobility. Stephen's father, Albert, became a high-school principal, and his mother, Marie (nee McAndrew), ran the language lab at a local college.

Growing up in a post-industrial age, young Stephen found nothing unusual about the gob piles, the mounds of blackened coal waste, that his family passed on the drive to visit his maternal grandmother. He took it for granted that the Lackawanna terminal, with its limestone facing and bronze clock, was a perpetual redevelopment project that had not welcomed an actual train since 1970. For that matter, all the abandoned and overgrown tracks and trestles around town seemed merely like great places for bike rides. Moving through high school, discovering a love for theater, Stephen lived almost oblivious to the story unfolding outside his front door, the story he was destined to tell.

Then he went to college at Brown University, a place so foreign to him he had never before heard the term WASP. "When you start to separate, you have this emotional connection to the place you grew up," he explained to me. "It's visceral, connected to the sights and sounds. Then you move away and you see your hometown the way the world does. I felt a protectiveness and a sadness about people seeing Scranton as a place that is wilting. Then Scranton becomes the stand-in for Slough in the American version of *The Office,* and you realize your hometown is the butt of jokes. I've taken friends back home and you feel it's a place that's depressed—the industry has left the building—but it's also home. So there's a comfort to it."

In that friction between the Scranton of sentimental memory and the Scranton of hardscrabble reality, Karam had found his subject and his subject had found him. He may have notionally set his first two professional plays in other places— Salem, Oregon, for *Speech & Debate*, and Nazareth, Pennsylvania, for *Sons of the Prophet*—but the psychic and topical terrain was plainly inspired by Karam's experience of Scranton. *Speech & Debate* (2006) portrayed three high-school students as they sought to expose a pedophiliac teacher; *Sons of the Prophet* (2011) focused on the gay son of a Lebanese-American Maronite Christian family, a scenario very much like the playwright's own. These works, with their darkly edged comedy, put Karam on the literary map. *Speech & Debate* became one of the most widely produced new plays of its decade on the regional-theater circuit, while *Sons of the Prophet* was a finalist for the 2012 Pulitzer Prize.

Like its predecessors, *The Humans* does not take place in Scranton. The narrative action, conveyed in ninety unbroken minutes of real time, occurs in the shabby apartment in Manhattan's Chinatown where Brigid Blake, the youngest child of her family, has just moved in with her boyfriend, Richard Saad. The couple is hosting Thanksgiving dinner for the rest of Brigid's family: her parents Erik and Deirdre, her older sister Aimee, her grandmother Momo.

With this ensemble, Karam takes on the challenge to which every major American playwright must rise, composing a family drama that speaks far beyond domestic concerns alone. Eugene O'Neill's *Long Day's Journey into Night* stands as the common ancestor and impossibly lofty standard for all the plays and playwrights to follow, from Tennessee Williams (*The Glass Menagerie*) to Arthur Miller (*All My Sons, Death of a Salesman*) to Sam Shepard (*A Lie of the Mind, Buried Child*) to Marsha Norman (*'night, Mother*) to Wendy Wasserstein (*The Sisters Rosensweig*) to August Wilson (*Fences, The Piano Lesson*).

At one level, Karam mines the relational conflicts of family life with both copious compassion and astringent wit. Aimee is heartbroken after a breakup with her lesbian lover and also afflicted with ulcerative colitis. Momo is deep into dementia, prone to explosions of angry gibberish. Deirdre and Erik, each in their way, plead with Brigid to marry Richard and, while she's at it, return to her lapsed Catholic faith. Karam's unerring ear for the Blake banter, the dueling jibes about everything from cockroaches to kale, has an audience laughing at nearly every line.

The kitchen-sink setting and abundant punchlines, though, serve to set a trap. For the deeper subject that Karam means to plumb concerns the Blakes not only as amusingly fallible individuals but as people being acted upon by larger societal forces. "I never set out to write an 'issue' play," Karam told me, referring to a label some critics have hung on *The Humans*, intending it as a compliment. "I wrote the play because I wanted to air out what was in my mind. The reason you create is because there's a story crawling to get out of you. The same thing that's keeping you up at night, you hope others will care about."

Perhaps coincidentally, perhaps not, Karam started writing *The Humans* in 2012, soon after the Occupy Wall Street movement forced the discussion of income inequality onto the front page. He kept writing, even as it appeared that Occupy had stricken its tent cities and vanished without an impact. And he kept writing before Bernie Sanders and Donald Trump launched presidential campaigns that, in almost irreconcilable ways, gave vent to populist resentment and rage.

The Blakes do not rage. Yet in the spikiest bits of Karam's dialogue they give voice to people who are teetering on the edge of the elevator shaft. An exchange like this one makes Karam's audience gasp with both humor and somber recognition.

BRIGID

I'm spending most of my nights bartending—you guys don't even know how much student debt I'm stuck with—

ERIK

Yeah, well, I *do* know who refused to go to a state school.

As we learn, Erik has been stuck as a high-school maintenance man for twenty-eight years. Deirdre, an office manager, laments, "I'm working for two more guys in their twenties, and just 'cause they have a special degree they're making five times what I make, over forty years I've been there." With the family affluence that supports his graduate-school studies in social work, Richard abrades the Blakes' fragile esteem all the more by his sincere efforts at kinship. At one point, recounting his bout with depression, Richard tells Erik how grateful he is for being able to "re-boot" his life. To which Erik responds, "Doing life twice sounds like the only thing worse than doing it once."

Karam is too much a humanist to reduce the Blakes to the sum of their victimization. As strapped as the parents are—Erik cuts his own hair to save money—Deirdre volunteers to help Bhutanese refugees whose poverty touches her conscience. And the most crushing blow in the Blakes' lives, and thus in the play, comes from a personal failing (not to be revealed here). But with his great heart and expansive social vision, Karam understands, and makes an audience understand, that while anyone can commit such a mistake, people from the nation's many Scrantons don't have the security to survive it whole. And, forget about the zombies, a life without any margin for error is its own kind of waking, walking death.

Samuel G. Freedman is a columnist for the New York Times, a journalism professor at Columbia University, and the author of eight books.

THE
HUMANS

PRODUCTION HISTORY

The Humans was commissioned by the Roundabout Theatre Company and received its world premiere on November 18, 2014, at the American Theater Company (PJ Paparelli, Artistic Director) in Chicago. It was directed by PJ Paparelli; the set design was by David Ferguson, the costume design was by Brittany Dee Bodley, the lighting design was by Brian Hoehne, the sound design was by Patrick Bley; the production stage manager was Amanda J. Davis, the production manager was Markie Gray and the assistant stage manager was Abigail Medrano. The cast was:

ERIK BLAKE	Keith Kupferer
DEIRDRE BLAKE	Hanna Dworkin
AIMEE BLAKE	Sadieh Rifai
BRIGID BLAKE	Kelly O'Sullivan
"MOMO" BLAKE	Jean Moran
RICHARD SAAD	Lance Baker

The Humans received its New York premiere at the Roundabout Theatre Company (Todd Haimes, Artistic Director; Harold Wolpert, Managing Director; Julia C. Levy, Executive Director; Sydney Beers, General Manager) on October 26, 2015. It was directed by Joe Mantello; the set design was by David Zinn, the costume design was by Sarah Laux, the lighting design was by Justin Townsend, the sound design was by Fitz Patton; the artistic consultant was Robyn Goodman, the literary manager was Jill Rafson, the production stage manager was William Joseph Barnes and the associate stage manager was Devin Day. The cast was:

ERIK BLAKE	Reed Birney
DEIRDRE BLAKE	Jayne Houdyshell
AIMEE BLAKE	Cassie Beck
BRIGID BLAKE	Sarah Steele
"MOMO" BLAKE	Lauren Klein
RICHARD SAAD	Arian Moayed

The Humans opened on Broadway at The Helen Hayes Theatre on February 18, 2016. The producers were Scott Rudin, Barry Diller, Roundabout Theatre Company, Fox Theatricals, James L. Nederlander, Terry Allen Kramer, Roy Furman, Daryl Roth, Jon B. Platt, Eli Bush, Broadway Across America, Jack Lane, Barbara Whitman, Jay Alix and Una Jackman, Scott M. Delman, Sonia Friedman, Amanda Lipitz, Peter May, Stephanie P. McClelland, Lauren Stein, The Shubert Organization; Joey Parnes, Sue Wagner, John Johnson, executive producers. The artistic team and cast remained the same as the Roundabout production.

DRAMATIS PERSONAE

ERIK BLAKE, sixty

DEIRDRE BLAKE, Erik's wife, sixty-one

AIMEE BLAKE, their daughter, thirty-four

BRIGID BLAKE, their daughter, twenty-six

"MOMO" BLAKE, Erik's mother, seventy-nine

RICHARD SAAD, Brigid's boyfriend, thirty-eight

NOTES

1. A slash (/) means the character with the next line of dialogue begins his or her speech.

2. Dialogue in brackets [ ] is expressed nonverbally.

3. *The Humans* takes place in one real-time scene—on a two-level, four-room set—with no blackouts. Life continues in all spaces at all times. While this is difficult to render on the page, the noting of "**UPSTAIRS**" v. "**DOWNSTAIRS**" is a reminder of the exposed "dollhouse" view the audience has at all times. Throughout the journey, the audience's focus may wander into whichever room it chooses.

There are six basic fears, with some combination of
which every human suffers at one time or another . . .
The fear of *poverty*
The fear of *criticism*
The fear of *ill health*
The fear of *loss of love of someone*
The fear of *old age*
The fear of *death*

—NAPOLEON HILL, *THINK AND GROW RICH*

The subject of the "uncanny" . . . belongs to all that
is terrible—to all that arouses dread and creeping horror . . . The German word [for "uncanny"], *unheimlich*, is obviously the opposite of *heimlich* . . . meaning "familiar," "native," "belonging to the home"; and
we are tempted to conclude that what is "uncanny" is
frightening precisely because it is *not* known and familiar . . . [But] among its different shades of meaning the
word *heimlich* exhibits one which is identical with its
opposite, *unheimlich* . . . on the one hand, it means that
which is familiar and congenial, and on the other, that
which is concealed and kept out of sight.

—SIGMUND FREUD, *THE UNCANNY*

The mask. Look at the mask!
Sand, crocodile, and fear above New York.

—FEDERICO GARCÍA LORCA, *DANCE OF DEATH*

A *turn-of-the-century ground-floor/basement duplex tenement apartment in New York City's Chinatown. It's just big enough to not feel small. It's just small enough to not feel big.*

The two floors are connected via a spiral staircase. Each floor has its own entrance.

The apartment's pre-war features have been coated in layers of faded off-white paint, rendering the space curiously monotone. The rooms are worn, the floors are warped, but clean and well kept.

The layout doesn't adhere to any sensible scheme; the result of a mid-century renovation in which two autonomous apartments were combined.

UPSTAIRS:
Two rooms divided by an open entryway. The room with the staircase also has the apartment's lone, large deep-set window with bars. The window gets no direct sunlight. An urban recliner is the only piece of furniture upstairs. The other room has a door that leads to the duplex's sole bathroom.

DOWNSTAIRS:

Two windowless rooms divided by an even larger open entry-way—with a different floorplan than upstairs. A small kitchen alley is wedged awkwardly behind the spiral staircase. The other room is dominated by a modest folding table. The table is set with six paper plates and napkins with turkeys on them. Plastic silver-ware. Scattered moving boxes. Not much else.

The apartment is a touch ghostly, but not in a forced manner; empty pre-war basement apartments are effortlessly uncanny.

At lights:

Erik is upstairs, alone, some plastic bags in his hands. Beside him is an empty wheelchair. He takes in the space. The main door is open. Beat.

A sickening THUD sounds from above the ceiling. Erik looks up.

ERIK

[What the hell was that?]

He recovers.

Gradually his attention shifts away from the noise; he continues to explore the space when—

Another sickening THUD sounds from above, startling him. He looks up.

ERIK

[God, what the hell is that?]

A toilet flush.

Aimee and Brigid enter through the main door carrying a few plastic bags.

AIMEE

This is the last of the goodies . . .

(to Erik)
I told you guys not to bring anything.

Deirdre and Momo exit the bathroom; Momo is shaky on her feet.

Erik helps her into her wheelchair.

DEIRDRE
Mission accomplished . . .

BRIGID   ERIK
It's pretty big, right?   I gotcha, Mom, there you go . . .

AIMEE
Definitely bigger than your last place.

ERIK
Is there some kinda construction going on upstairs?

BRIGID
Oh, no that's our neighbor, we think she drops stuff? Or stomps around?—we don't know . . .

DOWNSTAIRS:
Richard emerges from the kitchen alley.

RICHARD
(calling up)
Everyone okay up there?

BRIGID
We're fine, babe, just keep an eye on the oven, we'll be down in a minute.

RICHARD
You got it.

ERIK
Have you complained to her about the noise?

BRIGID

No, Dad, she's a seventy-year-old Chinese woman, / I'm not gonna—

DEIRDRE

Well, Brigid, I'm sixty-one—older people can still process information, we're / still able to—

BRIGID

I'm saying she means well, she's older so I don't wanna disturb her if I don't have to / . . . hey, here, I'll take your coats . . .

MOMO

(mumbled)
You can never come back . . . you can never come back / . . . you can never come back . . . cannevery you come back . . .

DEIRDRE

All right . . . you're all right, Mom . . .

Momo's mumbling is not directed to anyone—her primary focus is down, toward the floor, lost; she is passive and disconnected.

BRIGID

What's she saying?

DEIRDRE   MOMO

She's—[who the hell knows]—   . . . fernall here sullerin . . .
even when she *is* saying real   werstrus um black . . . sezz it
stuff . . . what's been coming   bigger . . . fernal down /
out is still all . . . [muddled] . . .   black . . . sorn it all . . .

ERIK

Mom, hey Mom, this is Brigid's new apartment . . .

BRIGID

How are you, Momo?

DEIRDRE

We're gonna have Thanksgiving at your granddaughter's new place, / that sound good?

(mumbled)
. . . you can never come back . . . you can never come back . . .

BRIGID
Momo, you can absolutely come back, any time you want.

Deirdre moves into the room with the recliner.

ERIK
This is a decent layout, Bridge . . . / good space . . .

DEIRDRE
Really nice . . .

BRIGID
It's good, right?—I can set up my music workspace downstairs so I won't drive Rich crazy.

DEIRDRE
This is a fancy chair . . . Erik, check out this fancy chair . . .

ERIK
I thought all your furniture was on the moving truck.

BRIGID
It is—Richard's parents gave us that—a couch, too . . . we're not sure if the living area'll be up here or—this might become the bedroom . . .

AIMEE
(noticing the staircase)
I can't believe you have a downstairs . . .

ERIK
Why would they give something this nice away?

BRIGID	MOMO
Because they got a new one, Dad.	*(softly mumbled)* . . . fernall all sertrus inner . . .

(referring to the recliner)
You might want something even bigger up here . . .

BRIGID

This isn't Scranton, I don't need an oversized recliner in every room.

MOMO
(mumbled)
. . . you can never come back . . . you can never come back . . .

Erik is drawn to the window, studies the surroundings.

BRIGID

Momo . . . ?

DEIRDRE

It's her latest phrase-of-the-day . . . the doctor says it's normal, the repeating . . .

BRIGID

And . . . how's she been?

Eriks stops staring out the window.
Momo's face remains blank and focused on the floor.

ERIK

Uh . . . she's still got her good days, you know? . . . yesterday she was pretty with it for most of the morning, but now she's [all over the place] . . . I dunno where she goes . . .

DEIRDRE

I tried to do her hair, I want her to look good, / you know?

AIMEE	BRIGID
She does . . .	Treat yourself to a spa day . . .
	/ the both of you should go—

DEIRDRE

No, no way, do you know how much that costs?

STEPHEN KARAM

Yeah, well you'll burn out if you're / not careful—

Hey, hey don't worry about us—having her at home with us is, until it becomes too much, it's a blessing, you know . . . right Erik? . . . Erik . . .

Erik has been staring out the window again—something outside caught his attention.

Dad— / come back to earth . . .

Sorry, sorry . . . long drive.

BRIGID	ERIK
Are you okay?	Yeah, once I get some caffeine in me, I'll be good . . .

(trying to find the light switch in the bathroom)
Hey is the light switch . . . ?

No, it's on the outside . . .

Another THUD sounds above the ceiling. Erik is the only one who looks up.

You want me to call the super about the noise?—

No, no this is New York, people are loud, why are you so—

Hey, he had a rough night, he hasn't been sleeping, / he's been—Erik, you haven't . . .

BRIGID	ERIK
Why haven't you been sleeping?	Deirdre, c'mon . . . [please don't talk about this] . . .
Are you okay? . . .	*(to Brigid)*
	I'm—yeah, I'm okay . . .

AIMEE

(offstage, from behind the bathroom door)
There's no toilet paper!

BRIGID

Okay, hang on . . .

*Brigid searches for toilet paper in one of the boxes/shopping bags.
Deirdre follows her.*

ERIK

Hey you get cell reception in here?

BRIGID

Up here we do, if—is it a Verizon phone?

ERIK

Uh, Sprint.

BRIGID

Then you have to lean up against the window.

ERIK

In here? I wanna check the score of the game.

BRIGID

Yeah . . . but now, yeah, now lean in . . .

*Erik sits in the window ledge trying to get reception. Brigid looks
for toilet paper.*

DEIRDRE

The sheets were covered in sweat last night . . . I dunno if he's
having nightmares or what—

BRIGID

Rich sometimes takes a sleeping pill, I can ask him what kind
of / medicine—

DEIRDRE

Oh right like your dad'd ever try any sorta—no, no I bet . . . he'll
sleep better after seeing you guys today, it'll be good for him . . .

BRIGID

Okay . . . well, good . . .

*Brigid cracks the bathroom door open, hands Aimee the toilet
paper, then shuts the door.*

DEIRDRE

. . . yeah . . .

AIMEE

(offstage)
Thank you.

BRIGID

. . . and . . . how's Aimee? . . .

DEIRDRE

[I dunno] . . . she's still heartbroken, you know? . . .

BRIGID

[Yeah,] it's gonna be weird for *us*, not having Carol around . . .

DEIRDRE

Well I'm telling you if they got married it—

BRIGID

Mom . . .

DEIRDRE

—hey, it's why I don't like you
and Rich moving in together /
before making a real
commitment—

BRIGID

I know, Mom, but—

—marriage can help you weather a storm, / that's all—

BRIGID

—okay, but we put this to rest, / yeah? . . .

DEIRDRE

I know, yeah, I'm sorry.

MOMO

Sorn it allinners, /sorn it all . . .

BRIGID
(noticing Momo's runny nose)
Mom—Momo's nose . . .

DEIRDRE

Oh God . . .
(lovingly wiping Momo's nose)
. . . there we go, Mom, there we go . . .

ERIK

The Lions are up seven.

BRIGID   DEIRDRE
Yay . . .   Thank God, we can eat in peace.

BRIGID

Sorry you're not sleeping, Big Guy . . .

ERIK

I'm fine.

BRIGID

. . . do you want to put your feet up and take a quick nap before dinner?—

ERIK
(amused by her worry)
No way, are you kidding me?, / no . . .

BRIGID

I'm serious!

ERIK

. . . no, I'm good . . .

BRIGID

Rich hasn't been sleeping much either, he's been having weird dreams about—he thinks they're related to the stress of the move . . .

DEIRDRE

Oh man . . .

BRIGID

. . . yeah, and he's been keeping *me* up while he tries to unravel their meaning.

DEIRDRE

Why's he doing that?

BRIGID

He took *one* psychology course last year and suddenly he's an armchair psychiatrist.

RICHARD
(calling up)
I took *two* psychology courses!

BRIGID	DEIRDRE
[One.]	*(calling down)*
	Hey there, Rich! . . .

RICHARD	ERIK
(calling up)	
Hey, I'll be up in a minute! . . .	Bridge—hey . . . I keep noticing a lotta—you guys gotta caulk all along the molding down there . . . / there's big gaps there . . .

BRIGID

Thanks, okay, Repairman, thank you, but can you at least . . .
someone needs to say something about my big window. No one
has said anything about my big window . . .

DEIRDRE
(aside, to Erik)
I love seeing her this excited, don't you love seeing her / this
excited?

ERIK
Yeah, I do, we don't have to talk about it.

*Brigid walks into the area near the spiral staircase, searches for
something amidst the boxes.*

RICHARD
(calling up)
Honey, bring down the napkins, okay?

UPSTAIRS:	BRIGID
Unseen by Brigid, Deirdre	Richard, what are you yelling
and Erik confer about	at me?
something in the hallway	RICHARD
or next room.	I said: bring down the napkins
They are audible-but-	please!
indecipherable.	BRIGID
	Yeah, Richard, or you can get
	them yourself.
The tail end of their	
conversation:	
	RICHARD
DEIRDRE	Do you / want me to—
(audible-but-	
indecipherable)	
Okay, but / . . . if you wait—	BRIGID
okay, I just don't want—	*(meeting him halfway on*
	the stairs)
	No I got them, sorry . . .

ERIK
(audible-but-indecipherable)
Hey—gimme some space, I will . . . I will—

Brigid hears the tail end of Deirdre's private discussion with Erik.
Aimee exits the bathroom.

BRIGID
You guys better not be dissing my home—do you even get how special a place like this is? No New Yorkers have duplex apartments.

AIMEE
Except for the thousands of New Yorkers who have duplex apartments—

BRIGID
I *knew* you were gonna / say that—

AIMEE
Oh come on, I love it . . . / it's amazing . . .

ERIK   DEIRDRE
We all love it . . .   Me too, but . . . why are there
                                              bars on the window? Is the
                                              neighborhood dangerous?

BRIGID   AIMEE
No that's standard for a   *(smiling)*
ground-floor apartment—   Mom, no . . .

BRIGID
. . . after a while you don't even notice them—

DEIRDRE
Yeah, you don't notice them 'cause there's no sunlight in here . . .
/ it's like a cave . . .

BRIGID
Mom . . .

                              ERIK
        (looking out the window)
        Hey, who's walking around out there?

                              BRIGID
        Uh, must be the super, he's the only one who has access.

                              ERIK
        No, she's got gray hair?

                              BRIGID
        Lemme see . . . where?

        Erik looks back out the window; this time he sees nothing.

                              ERIK
        She went inside, I guess . . .

        Brigid moves away from the window.

                              BRIGID
        Probably the super's wife, I haven't met her yet.
        (to Erik, who is still staring out the window)
        Hey, Detective . . . sit down and relax.

                              DEIRDRE
        I wish you had more of a view—

                              BRIGID
        Mom . . .

                              DEIRDRE
        What?—it's an alley full of cigarette butts—

                              BRIGID
        It's an *interior courtyard* . . . / not a—

STEPHEN KARAM

ERIK	DEIRDRE
Oh, excuse me . . .	Well hey now, Fancy . . .
	perhaps we should all take a
	stroll in the interior courtyard
	after dinner.

Brigid sighs, she knows she can't win.

BRIGID

Okay, yes, it's gross smokers use the alley as their ashtray, but . . .
you don't think this place has potential?

ERIK

I think if you moved to Pennsylvania your quality of life would
shoot up.

BRIGID

Uh, if I moved to Pennsylvania, *your* quality of life would shoot
up / tremendously—

ERIK	DEIRDRE
Oh yeah?	*(smiling)*
	Don't flatter yourself, Lady . . .

ERIK

What makes you think we like you so much?

BRIGID

You drove in from Scranton in the snow—

ERIK

The roads are all plowed—

Brigid hugs Erik. Deirdre recognizes a box.

DEIRDRE

Is this our—Bridge, you didn't even *open* our care-package?

BRIGID

I'm not opening *anything* until the moving truck gets here—

ERIK

Is it in transit or / is it still—

BRIGID

No, no it's still stuck in Queens—Rich knows the details,
but—now with the parade traffic, they won't guarantee their
mechanic'll fix it before tomorrow . . .

*Brigid finds what she has been looking for: a bag with several
wrapped objects.*

DEIRDRE

What's all that?

BRIGID
(handing out the wrapped packages)

You guys went out of your way to get here, / so . . . open . . .

DEIRDRE

What is it? . . .

BRIGID

Open, open . . .

AIMEE   DEIRDRE

What did you get us?   Thank you . . . Erik don't
                                 [throw your wrapping away]—
                                 I wanna save the wrapping . . .

They each unwrap a framed photo.

ERIK

Oh man . . .

AIMEE   DEIRDRE

You gotta be kidding me . . .   Oh God . . .

Aimee laughs.

STEPHEN KARAM

24

ERIK

Wow . . .

BRIGID

Found it when I was packing.

DEIRDRE

. . . oh man . . . were we ever this young? . . . look how *young* you are, Aimee . . .

AIMEE

I'm an elephant in this photo . . .

DEIRDRE   BRIGID
You're beautiful.   No . . .

AIMEE

. . . and I'm holding a funnel cake . . . I can't even blame genetics . . .

ERIK

This is gold, Brigid, / thanks. Check it out, Mom . . .

DEIRDRE

It really is, honey . . . thank you.

AIMEE

I am a *planet* in this photo.

DEIRDRE   ERIK
Stop it, I'm bigger than you . . .   You look beautiful.

DEIRDRE

I miss Wildwood . . .

BRIGID   ERIK
Go back, take a vacation . . .   Oh man, that boardwalk . . .

DEIRDRE

Talk to this one, he hates traveling—

ERIK

I do not / hate traveling—

BRIGID

You hate traveling to New York—

ERIK

I do not hate traveling to New / York, no, no, I don't . . .

DEIRDRE   AIMEE
Yes you do!   Okay, that's a lie.

ERIK

. . . I *hate* that you're moving a few blocks from where two tow-
ers got blown up and in a major flood zone . . . / I hate *that* . . .

BRIGID

This area is safe—

ERIK

Chinatown *flooded* during the last hurricane— / it flooded—

BRIGID

Yeah, that's why I can afford to live here—it's not like you gave
me any money to help me out.

ERIK   BRIGID
Wow . . .   Hey, I'm—sorry, just . . .
                                           Chinatown is safe— / you saw
                                           my block, Dad—

DEIRDRE

Of course it is . . .

BRIGID

—no one's gonna steer a plane into a, a fish market on Grand
Street—

AIMEE   DEIRDRE
Brigid . . .   Let it go . . .

ERIK
I liked you living in Queens, all right? I worry enough with
Aimee on the top floor of the Cira Centre—

AIMEE
Well stop, Philly is more stable than New York—

BRIGID
Aimee, don't / make him more—

AIMEE
I'm just saying—it's safer . . .

BRIGID
Yeah, 'cause not even terrorists wanna spend time in Philly, /
Philly is awful—

AIMEE
Oh, ha ha . . .

ERIK
You think everything's awful, you think *Scranton* is awful, / but
it's the place that—

BRIGID   AIMEE
We *think* it's awful?!   Dad, it is!

ERIK
(their amusement forces him to smile)
. . . yeah, well what *I* think's funny is how you guys, you move to
big cities and trash Scranton, when Momo almost killed herself
getting outta New York—she didn't have a real toilet in this city,
and now her granddaughter moves right back to the place / she
struggled to escape . . .

BRIGID
We know, yes . . . "return to the slums" . . .

DEIRDRE
It's not the slums anymore . . .

ERIK

Oh man, that store—on the corner of Eldridge?—we went in to
get you a candle—

DEIRDRE

Don't *tell* her that, Erik, we didn't end up buying it—

ERIK

The most expensive candles I've ever seen in my life.

AIMEE

(*a gentle reality check*)
They were twenty-five dollars.

ERIK   DEIRDRE

That's a lot of money!   For a *candle*?! That's insane,
                                              you should get five candles for
                                              that . . .

*Richard ascends the staircase with a bottle of champagne and
plastic cups.*

RICHARD

Hey, thought we could have a champagne toast up here? Brigid
claims we need to bless the upstairs *and* downstairs . . .

DEIRDRE   BRIGID

That is good Irish tradition,   Yes, thanks, babe.
yessir . . .

AIMEE

Should we sing Momo's favorite / —we have to, right? . . .

BRIGID

Of course we're gonna sing it! Rich has been warned.

*Under the following dialogue, Erik wanders into the adjoining
room to grab a private moment for himself; he rubs his aching
lower back, takes a deep breath.*

In the other room, Richard pours champagne into the plastic cups.

We only have plastic cups, but the good news is the bar is set very low if we ever host again.

AIMEE

We could care less . . .

DEIRDRE

Thank you, Richard . . . champagne'll make the cups feel fancy.

Erik enters the bathroom.

BRIGID

Dad . . . ?

Brigid pokes her head into the other room, sees the shut bathroom door.

AIMEE

Did he sleep at *all* last night?

BRIGID

Yeah he seems—

DEIRDRE

I'm not gonna worry about him, okay, otherwise / I'll stop sleeping myself . . .

AIMEE

Okay, okay . . .

BRIGID

All right, let's just, let's show Rich how badly our voices blend, / we'll do the money verses, yeah? . . .

RICHARD

I'm excited to hear this . . .

AIMEE

Yeah, and FYI, I've been staying on key lately, you need to calm down . . .

DEIRDRE

The Blakes have been singing it for generations.

BRIGID

You need to calm down . . .

THE HUMANS

29

Will Momo join in if we—

Oh yeah—she's still good with music, Rich, wait'll you hear, /
she'll join in . . .

BRIGID
(calling to the bathroom)
—Dad! We're waiting for you . . .
(to Aimee)
. . . you want to start us off ? . . .

AIMEE
No, no . . . I always start too high and you yell at me.

Erik exits the bathroom and starts to sing.

ERIK
Oh all / the money that ere I had—

BRIGID   *Erik's singing elicits groans*
Oh my God . . .   *from the women.*

BRIGID
Get in here! That is a terrible key for me. Okay, Momes . . .

Erik joins the group in the next room. Brigid takes Momo's hand,
sings to her.

BRIGID
(restarting in a better key for her)
Oh all the money that ere I had,
I lost it in good company

(spoken)
Ladies . . . [join me] . . .

They look to Momo affectionately, expecting her to join in.

STEPHEN KARAM

BRIGID, AIMEE AND DEIRDRE
And of all the harm that ere I've done,
Alas was done to none but me
And all I've done for want of wit,
To memory now I can't recall

BRIGID
[Dad, you sing too . . .]

BRIGID, AIMEE, DEIRDRE AND ERIK
Lay down your fears and raise your glass
May peace and joy be with you all

Momo remains blank.

DEIRDRE   ERIK
Aimee, take a verse . . .   . . . yeah, you go, Aimee . . .

AIMEE
Oh may all the friends that ere I had,
They'd be sorry at my going away

(spoken)
I'm a lawyer, Rich—

(back to singing)
And may all the sweethearts that e'er I had . . . [Guys, sing
with me please . . .]

BRIGID, AIMEE AND DEIRDRE
They would wish me one more day to stay

Erik, sensing Aimee's sadness, takes over.

ERIK
And if I had money enough to spend
And leisure time to sit a while
(indicating Deirdre)
There is a maiden in this town
Who sorely has my heart beguiled

Yeah, it better be me.

ERIK AND BRIGID
Her pale white cheeks her skin of snow,
I will not rest till she comes to call

BRIGID
Take it home . . .

BRIGID, AIMEE, DEIRDRE AND ERIK
Lay down your fears and raise your glass.
May peace and joy be with you all.

They ad-lib cheers, drink. The joy of the song is cut short by Momo's steady mumbling.

MOMO
. . . nairywheres do we blag werstrus, doll sezzer / big sussten back . . . sezz it whairidoll . . . er hairin sildern fernal garn ackening ery or loddinsezz . . .
(tapering to quiet under the family's conversation)
. . . nairywheres do we blag werstrus, doll sezzer big sussten back . . . sezz it whairidoll . . . er hairin sildern fernal garn ackening ery or loddinsezz . . .

ERIK
(staying positive, massaging Momo's hand)
Shhhh, all right . . . you're all right . . .

BRIGID
She normally joins in. This is new, / this is—

ERIK
Well it's—yeah, it's not one of her good days.

Small beat.

DEIRDRE
I've missed hearing you sing, Bridge . . .

BRIGID	DEIRDRE
Mom, / that's not even my strength . . .	. . . I'm serious, you sound good—

ERIK	RICHARD
You have any gigs lined up? Can we come embarrass you?—	*(to Deirdre)* I agree.

BRIGID
No, I'm spending most of my nights bartending—you guys don't even know how much student debt I'm stuck with—

ERIK
Yeah, well, I *do* know who refused to go to a state school.

DEIRDRE	BRIGID
Ohhh, score one for Dad.	I knew you were gonna say that . . .

RICHARD
Why don't we—appetizers are out, / so just come down whenever you're ready . . .

BRIGID
Yes, good idea—let's move the party downstairs—

Everyone gathers their things, starts to move. Another THUD from above.

Erik looks up; everyone else keeps moving. Brigid notices this.

BRIGID
(to Erik)
Hey . . . it's quieter down there . . . come down and unwind.

Brigid heads toward the stairwell. Richard arrives downstairs.

Deirdre heads for the bathroom. Erik is still preoccupied with the noise, looking up.

Brigid stops, she's noticed Erik isn't behind her. She turns and sees him staring at the ceiling.

                    BRIGID
Dad, what're you doing?—go downstairs and relax, / please—

        ERIK   DEIRDRE
All right, okay . . .   I am, just gonna use the little
                             girls' room first . . .

                    AIMEE
How do I get Momo down there? . . .

                    BRIGID
What do you mean?

                    AIMEE
Well I can't dump her down the spiral staircase.

                    BRIGID
Oh God, sorry, use the elevator—

        ERIK   AIMEE
Here, I'll take her—   *(taking control of the*
                              wheelchair)
                             I got it, I never get to see her . . .
                             go help Rich . . .

                    ERIK
You sure?

                    AIMEE
Yeah . . .

Erik heads downstairs. Brigid opens the door for Aimee and Momo.

                    BRIGID
Take the elevator to the B-level.

DOWNSTAIRS:
Erik descends the spiral staircase. Richard is making last-minute dinner preparations.

BRIGID

(calling down)
Rich, unlock the downstairs door please!

RICHARD

(calling up)
You got it!

ERIK

Look at all this . . .

RICHARD

Come on down . . .

UPSTAIRS:

DEIRDRE

So when Momo needs the bathroom we've gotta go out in the hall and take the elevator?

BRIGID

Yeah, but . . . *I'll* take her back up if . . .
(Deirdre sighs)
Sorry, I forgot about her wheelchair.

DEIRDRE

Yeah, I know you did.

Deirdre enters the bathroom. Brigid heads for the staircase.

DOWNSTAIRS:
Erik looks around, investigating.

RICHARD

(handing Erik a beer)
Beer?

ERIK

Yeah, I'll take a Coke, too, if you've got / soda or . . .

RICHARD

Yeah, coming right up . . .

ERIK

Thanks. Detroit's up seven.

RICHARD

Oh . . . oh, the football game?
  (*Erik nods*)
How's the lake house coming along? I hear you might build this summer?

ERIK

Uh, no, not until the sewers get put in . . . doesn't make sense to build with a septic system if they're gonna be putting in sewers soon.

BRIGID

  (*coming down the stairs*)
The sooner the better, I can't wait for a lake-house Christmas.

RICHARD

  (*handing her a glass of wine*)
Red, right?

BRIGID

Yes, thank you . . .
  (*referring to the paper plates*)
. . . How do you like our fine china, Dad?

Erik smiles. Richard sets things out on the table, Brigid assists.

ERIK

You're gonna miss the old house.

BRIGID

I will; I won't miss the wall-to-wall carpeting . . . or the bunk beds.

Small beat. Erik drinks. Richard and Brigid prepare food in the kitchen alley.

RICHARD

Work's good, Erik?—you're still at—it's a Catholic high school, right?

BRIGID

St. Paul's, for twenty-eight years . . .

RICHARD

Wow, / that's impressive . . .

ERIK

Well . . .

BRIGID

They created a whole position for him.

ERIK

Don't make it sound—I headed up maintenance and coupla years ago they needed a, an equipment manager, so—

BRIGID

It's a big job, it's a triple-A school, he handles all the phys-ed classes, / manages the weight room, the kids love him . . .

ERIK

All right, okay . . . hey enough . . .

RICHARD

That's impressive.

ERIK

It's practical. Got the girls free tuition. You don't pick up after other people's kids for twenty-eight years unless you really love your own, you know?

RICHARD

(toasting)
Well, hey, to twenty-eight years . . .

BRIGID	**ERIK**
Twenty-eight years . . .	Cheers.

UPSTAIRS:
Toilet flush.

DOWNSTAIRS:
Brigid—who was waiting for the bathroom to be free—starts up the staircase.

RICHARD
Yeah, no it's crazy, our generation, we're lucky if we stay in a job for *one* year, right Bridge?

ERIK
Are you guys even *in* the same generation?

BRIGID
Dad, that's / not funny—

ERIK
What, I'm not allowed to joke?

BRIGID
No.

UPSTAIRS:
Deirdre exits the bathroom.

DOWNSTAIRS:
Richard continues meal preparations.

RICHARD
You decide on an architect for the lake house?

ERIK
Uh, no, that's a ways away.

Erik drinks.

(*arriving upstairs, seeing Deirdre*)
Hey . . .

DEIRDRE
Your bathroom doesn't have a window . . .

BRIGID   DEIRDRE
I know, go downstairs.   . . . I love you, I'm just saying.

Brigid enters the bathroom.
Deirdre goes into the other upstairs room to get her purse, she
pulls out two wrapped presents. She moisturizes her hands. At
some point on her way back to the stairs, she stops to eavesdrop
on Richard and Erik's conversation.

RICHARD
I actually like having the design process to look forward to, I like
the planning stages.

ERIK
Yeah, well our budget's—we're gonna use one of those places
where, they've got predesigned homes you can choose from? /
. . . but . . .

RICHARD
Sure, good idea . . .

ERIK
. . . yeah, and the place we're looking at has *good* designs, you
know? . . .

RICHARD
Yeah, no that's great.

Richard prepares for dinner during the following exchange. He's
listening, but multitasking.

ERIK

I'll tell you, Rich, save your money now . . . I thought I'd be
settled by my age, you know, but man, it never ends . . . mort-
gage, car payments, internet, our dishwasher just gave out . . .

RICHARD

Oh man . . .

ERIK

Yeah, yeah . . .
    (*small beat*)
. . . don'tcha think it should cost less to be alive?

RICHARD

Ha, absolutely . . .

ERIK

I even started cutting my own hair to try and save a few bucks . . .
messed it up pretty good. Thank God I'm married.

Richard smiles. Erik drinks. Beat.

RICHARD   ERIK
So you want—no, sorry what?   Brigid said you're—

ERIK

[Nothing, nevermind.]

Erik drinks.

RICHARD

You want some ice?

ERIK

Uh, sure.

RICHARD

   (*getting the ice*)
So you've been . . . having some weird dreams too?

Huh?

RICHARD

. . . just . . . you can hear a lot through the [hole where the spiral staircase is], just caught that you haven't been sleeping, thought maybe—I've been having weird dreams all week, think it's because of the move . . . last night I was polishing a silver refrigerator and . . . my dog was caught inside it? . . . and I don't have a dog? / . . . just weird stuff . . .

ERIK

Oh man . . . sounds like it . . . no, I don't remember my [dreams] . . . even when I have one of those ones where, uh . . .

Erik takes a sip of beer.

RICHARD

What?

ERIK

. . . [no, nothing important] . . . you know the ones where you need a minute just to . . . figure out it isn't / actually [real] . . .

RICHARD

Oh, sure—

Knocking at the downstairs door startles Erik a bit—he spills his beer. Richard moves to help—

ERIK   RICHARD
Sorry about that, Rich, I got   Don't worry about it—
it, I got it . . .

More knocking. Richard opens the door as Erik cleans up his spill. Aimee wheels Momo inside.

RICHARD

Welcome . . . / come on in . . .

                              AIMEE
Hello, hello . . . so this is what lies beneath . . .

                             RICHARD
What are you drinking, Aimee?

          AIMEE   MOMO
Whatever's open . . . red   *(barely audible)*
wine? This is really a lot of   . . . where do we go . . . where
space . . .   do we go . . .

                             RICHARD
Yeah if you sacrifice sunlight you can get some / extra square
feet . . .

                              MOMO
    (softly, mumbled)
Where do we go? Where, where do we go? / Where do we go?
Where do we go where do we go where do we go where do we
go . . .

                              ERIK
Hey, you waking up a bit, Mom? . . .

                              AIMEE
She keeps asking me that . . . Momo we're going into this room
is where we're going . . .

UPSTAIRS:
*Brigid exits the bathroom, is surprised to find Deirdre by the stair-
well.*

                             BRIGID
What are you doing? . . .

          DEIRDRE   MOMO
Just wanted a breather . . .   *(tapering to barely audible)*
                                 . . . where do we go do we go
                                 where do we go do we go . . .

Erik massages Momo's hand.

You're holding a present.

Ha, I am, it's for you and Rich. Open it downstairs . . .

Is it . . . a fancy candle?

Yeah, smart-ass, I'll give you a fancy candle . . . keep walking . . .

DOWNSTAIRS:
Aimee unwinds with a glass of wine.

How's the law firm, Aimee?

Busy. M&A transactions are not a source of joy in my life, so—
I'm glad you don't get cell reception down here, my blackberry
needs the rest.

She's an all-star there . . .

Dad, ugh, no—I was informed last month I'm no longer on the
partner track, which—

(descending the staircase)
What? / When did this—

Does that mean it just takes more time? Or—

No, it's the nice way of saying: start looking for another job.

THE HUMANS

DEIRDRE	ERIK
Why would they / do that?—	Really?

AIMEE

It's complicated, / who knows . . .

BRIGID

I'm sorry.

AIMEE

. . . yeah, I missed a lot of time last year when I was sick . . . /
and then . . .

DEIRDRE

She's got ulcerative colitis, Rich—

AIMEE

. . . Mom, okay—

DEIRDRE

—it affects the colon—

AIMEE

. . . okay, Mom, so . . . and I missed even *more* time right before
they made their decision, I had another flare-up this month,
so—

DEIRDRE	ERIK
Why didn't you tell us?	Oh babe, I'm sorry . . .

AIMEE

Because I don't want you to worry—

DEIRDRE

I would've sent you a care-package . . .

AIMEE

Yeah, and a bunch of text messages asking about my bowel
movements.

I just wanna know what's / going on.

ERIK   AIMEE
You know we'd do anything   I know, I know . . . I know,
for you, right?—   I do . . .

DEIRDRE
They can't fire you because of a medical condition—

AIMEE
Well they gave other reasons, obviously, but . . . yeah, you get
the sense they support your chronic illness as long as it doesn't
affect your billable hours.

BRIGID   DEIRDRE
I'm really sorry.   Well, they don't deserve you.

ERIK
How about . . . financially, are you okay, or—?

AIMEE
Yeah, I'm set for a while.

ERIK
For a few months, or—

AIMEE
Yeah, I'll let you know if I need money, I don't want to talk
about my job or my— / let's talk about—

DEIRDRE
But just—how are you feeling?

AIMEE
Just minor cramping, I'm good, I am . . .

RICHARD
How about food-wise, can we get you / something special—

AIMEE

No, I'm fine, at ease, everyone, / really . . . let's . . .

BRIGID

(taking the spotlight off Aimee)
Hey we should—why don't we do a downstairs toast, / before we forget, yeah? . . .

DEIRDRE   AIMEE

I'm okay with that . . .   Yes, / please . . .

BRIGID

Dad, will you lead us? . . .

RICHARD   ERIK

I like this, being twice   Sure, sure, how about . . .
blessed . . .

ERIK

. . . to the Blake Family Thanksgiving . . .

DEIRDRE

. . . to the very special Chinatown edition / of the Blake Family
Thanksgiving . . .

BRIGID   AIMEE

Yes, yes, yes . . .   Here here . . .

ERIK   MOMO

Neither rain nor hail—   Sorn it all . . .

DEIRDRE

Nor sleet nor snow . . .   . . . can neverbody black
nor . . . what else?   werstrus—

AIMEE

Nor ulcerative colitis . . .

MOMO

(mumbled)
. . . can neverbody black werstrus—

Nor dementia . . .

—you / sornum never back . . .

DEIRDRE   AIMEE
Okay, now you're pushing   Brigid . . .
it . . .

BRIGID
(smiling)
What—too soon? / Too soon?

AIMEE   DEIRDRE
Yes, too soon . . .   Not funny . . .

Brigid hugs Momo.

ERIK
Yeah, you *better* give her a hug . . .

BRIGID
We love you, Momes . . .

ERIK
To knowing this is what matters, right here . . . 'cause lemme
tell you, coming down these streets, thinking about how far the
Blakes've come . . . even seeing that candle store / was . . .

BRIGID
It's not a candle store, it's a boutique that sells, like, *one* candle—

ERIK
. . . hey I'm just appreciating how, you see all these rich people walking around New York, God knows where their money
comes from, but . . . end of the day, everything that *anyone's*
got . . . I don't care how many candles you have . . . one day it
goes . . . whatever gifts God's given us, in the end, no matter
who you are . . . everything you have *goes.*

Small beat.

> DEIRDRE

Well that's the *positive* way of looking at things.

Erik smiles.

> ERIK

Sorry—I love my family . . . / that's the short version, I'm glad we're together.

AIMEE	BRIGID
We love you too . . .	Love you guys . . .

DEIRDRE	RICHARD
Here here, amen . . .	Cheers . . .

> ERIK

And a special thanks to Richard for making this meal possible, since we know what a lousy cook Brigid is . . .

BRIGID	AIMEE
This is true . . .	Amen.

They all ad-lib "cheers" and toast.

> RICHARD

Okay, five minutes and everything will be out and ready to go . . .
  (setting out more food)
Here's some more munchies, here . . .

> DEIRDRE

Yum . . . thank you . . .

They all settle in. Erik looks after Momo.

> AIMEE

So how are you, Mom?

DEIRDRE

I'm good, I'm good . . . I was—did you get the text I sent about—
Bridge, this girl who played basketball for Dunmore, she was
bullied for being gay . . . her mom found her dead in her room
on Tuesday . . .

BRIGID	AIMEE
Whoa . . .	Oh man . . .

DEIRDRE

. . . yeah, suicide with some kinda pills . . . it's all over the news . . .
I texted you, / I wasn't sure if you got it?

AIMEE

This week was crazy . . . no, yeah I got it, I'm just behind with
my messages . . .

Deirdre picks at the crudités platter.

BRIGID

You don't have to text her every time a lesbian kills herself.

DEIRDRE	AIMEE
I don't.	She doesn't do that—
	I appreciate what / you're
	meaning . . .

DEIRDRE

I get enough annoying forwards myself, so—I don't wanna clog
up your guys's inbox—

AIMEE

You're not, Mom. You're good though?

DEIRDRE

I am, yeah . . . my bosses are—I'm an office manager, Rich, I've
been with the same company since right outta high school . . .

ERIK

Whole place would fall apart without her—

DEIRDRE

. . . yeah, well my *salary* doesn't reflect that, and these new kids they hired, I'm working for two more guys in their twenties, and just 'cause they have a special degree they're making five times what I make, over forty years / I've been there, Rich . . .

RICHARD
Wow, forty years . . . ?

BRIGID
Well . . . hey . . . focus on the lake house, you'll be able to unwind soon . . . you gotta take care of yourself.

AIMEE
Are you breaking ground this summer?

DEIRDRE
No . . .

RICHARD
It's smart to wait for the sewers, the value of your property will skyrocket.

AIMEE
When are they gonna be installed?

BRIGID
Thanks, Professor.

DEIRDRE
[I don't know . . .] Erik . . . ?

ERIK
That's up to the Department of Public Works, when the sewers get put in.

Small beat.

AIMEE
And how's Aunt Mary?

DEIRDRE

She's hanging in there, God love her . . . they got this contrap-
tion now to help load her into the pool but—Rich, this is their
aunt who had both knees replaced, / I drive her to her physical
therapy . . .

ERIK
(indicating the crudités platter)
Pass the . . .

DEIRDRE
. . . and did I e-mail you that—Kay Hoban has ovarian cancer . . .

AIMEE   BRIGID
Oh man, how's she doing?   She does? Yikes . . .

DEIRDRE
Yeah, I've been taking her to her treatments 'cause her and her
brother, they don't speak anymore, so . . . that's a whole mess,
but . . . she's being tough, so . . .
(takes a bite of food)
. . . what else . . . oh, Tuesdays I'm now—

BRIGID
Mom, you're talking with your mouth full.

Beat.

DEIRDRE
. . . I, uh, started volunteering for—Father Quinn told me about,
and don't roll your eyes, Erik . . .

ERIK
I'm not saying a word.

DEIRDRE
. . . right in Scranton there's a whole community of refugees
from Bhutan . . .

Aimee stifles laughter.

DEIRDRE
What? / It's not funny . . .

BRIGID
Let me guess, Saint Deirdre is coming to their rescue?—

ERIK
(smiling)
You have / no idea . . .

DEIRDRE
Be quiet—*you* have no idea—these people have *nothing* . . .
they're all just looking to learn English, to find work—we *think*
we've got nothing, but man . . .

RICHARD
That's great you're volunteering . . .

DEIRDRE
Thanks, Rich.

BRIGID
And how are *you,* Mom. Aimee didn't ask how the Republic of
Bhutan was doing—

ERIK	DEIRDRE
Hey, hey . . .	I'm *good*, smart-ass, I said that already . . . Now why don't you open your gift . . .

BRIGID	AIMEE
Mom, I was just teasing . . .	(getting up, registering a cramp) Hey guys—no one be alarmed if I'm up and down these stairs a million times to use the . . . facilities . . . so . . .

DEIRDRE
You want me to go with you?

Aimee shakes her head no as she goes up the stairs.
Brigid opens her gift, it's a small shiny pink pig.

BRIGID

. . . ah, it's a peppermint pig! Rich, check it out . . .

AIMEE	DEIRDRE
Amazing . . .	Hey, holler if we can do anything, okay?

AIMEE

(going up the stairs)
I will, don't smash that pig without me . . .

ERIK	DEIRDRE
We won't . . .	Poor baby . . .

BRIGID

And what is this other . . .
(opening the other wrapped object)
. . . ah, a Virgin Mary statue—

BRIGID	DEIRDRE
—complete with a serpent under her foot . . .	Okay, before you tease me, I know you guys don't believe, but she's appearing everywhere now not just in Fatima but in West Virginia and—just keep it for my sake, in the kitchen or even if you just put it in a drawer somewhere, okay?

BRIGID

Mom, I will absolutely put this in a drawer somewhere, / thank you.

DEIRDRE

Yeah, well . . . I feel better knowing you have it.

RICHARD

I thought maybe Brigid was making the pig-smash up, but—

ERIK

Oh no, it's real . . .

RICHARD	BRIGID
Can't wait to see how it works . . .	It's not Thanksgiving without it . . .
	(hugging Deirdre)
	. . . thank you.

DEIRDRE

You're welcome.

MOMO

(quietly, tapering to silence)
. . . why'm I hereson. Go warson herror truh. / Do the glassor comes blag . . . sezzor black . . . why'm I hereson. Go warson herror truh. Do the glassor comes blag . . . sezzor black . . . . . . why'm I hereson. Go warson herror truh. Do the glassor comes blag . . . sezzor black . . .

DEIRDRE

(massaging her hand)
Okay, okay, you wanna go for a ride, Mom? Let's go for a ride . . .

UPSTAIRS:
Aimee nurses a cramp before she proceeds to the bathroom.

DOWNSTAIRS:
Deirdre wheels Momo around the apartment.

ERIK

(to Brigid and Richard, referring to Momo)
She had a good day yesterday, you know? It's hard to predict now how she's gonna be . . . this is definitely her last big trip . . .

BRIGID

How are *you* doing? Is that why you aren't sleeping?—

ERIK	RICHARD
I'll sleep tonight—	Oh yeah, sorry Erik, we got sidetracked before—you were talking about your dream?

DEIRDRE

Oh, so you'll tell *him* details / about your dream—but you won't tell me?

RICHARD	ERIK
He didn't tell me details . . .	No—guys, I don't even remember it, there's nothing to tell . . .

BRIGID	DEIRDRE
Well, now I don't believe you . . .	I saw the way you woke up, don't tell me you can't remember something—

RICHARD	ERIK
(defending Erik)	*(smiling, to Brigid)*
Hey, no I forget mine if I don't write them down in the morning . . .	[Man, you're a piece of work.]

ERIK

See? . . . there you go . . .

DEIRDRE

Well whatever it was, couldn't a been scarier than the—
(laughing)
—I made him watch this—what was it called, Erik? . . . / the movie . . . ?

ERIK

What?

DEIRDRE

. . . the Lifetime movie about the housewife who got AIDS, / guys—it was so cheesy but really terrifying . . .

<table>
<tr><td>

BRIGID

Mom, you're steamrolling
the—

</td><td>

ERIK

She made me watch that . . .
(to Brigid)
Worst two hours of my life . . .

</td></tr>
</table>

DEIRDRE

You loved it.

RICHARD

What was scary about it?

DEIRDRE

This housewife cheats on her husband, right?—and he comes
home from work and asks her how her day was and—I mean
what can she say? "Today I cheated on you and contracted the
HIV-virus, honey, how was *your* day?" . . . can you *imagine*?

BRIGID

You're trying to be a comedian . . . / no more wine for you—

RICHARD

No, she's fine—be nicer to your mom, babe.

DEIRDRE

Thanks, Rich.

*Brigid goes to the kitchen, frustrated. Richard follows her. We
can glimpse them having a controlled-but-heated conversation.
Erik raises his eyebrows, tries to make light of this.*

DEIRDRE

Anything I say makes her [annoyed] . . .

ERIK

Yeah? Well who does she remind you of?

DEIRDRE

You.

ERIK

Me? She's all *you*, my
friend . . .

DEIRDRE

You, yeah you, my friend . . .

They smile at this disagreement.

DEIRDRE

Don't wait until after dinner.

Erik drinks his beer, thinks.

DEIRDRE

(getting up)
Your call, Big Guy . . .

Deirdre heads for the stairs. Brigid returns from the kitchen alley.

BRIGID

Where're you going?

DEIRDRE

Gonna check on Aimee—

BRIGID

I'll do it, stay down . . . stay down . . .

ERIK

Are her shakes in the fridge?

BRIGID

Yeah—Rich'll get it, sit down. Rich can you bring out an Ensure
shake? The straws are in the bag.

RICHARD

No problem.

ERIK

Thanks.

Brigid goes upstairs. Richard returns with an Ensure shake. Erik opens it, prepares the drink for Momo under the following. A bit awkward with just Erik, Deirdre and Richard.

DEIRDRE
So how's school, what is it a, a master's in social work you'll get?

RICHARD
Yeah, I have one more year . . .

UPSTAIRS:
Brigid knocks on the bathroom door.

BRIGID
You need anything?

AIMEE
(offstage)
An air freshener . . . ?

BRIGID
Just stink the place up. We'll deal.

AIMEE	MOMO
(offstage)	*(barely audible)*
I'll be out in a few.	I'm I here'm I why'm I here suh blag sezzor why'm I sezzor . . .
	(a bit louder)
	I'm I here'm I. / why'm I heresuh blag sezzor why'm I sezzor . . .

ERIK
You're here 'cause it's Thanksgiving, Mom, that's why you're here, Brigid invited us . . .

DOWNSTAIRS:
Richard continues dinner preparations during the following conversation.

RICHARD

Brigid said you guys went on a cruise last summer?

DEIRDRE

Yeah, we've gone on four of 'em now, to Halifax and Mexico . . . you ever been on one?

UPSTAIRS:
Brigid pauses at the top of the staircase to listen . . .

RICHARD

Uh, not on one of those big ships, but . . . I sailed with my family growing up.

ERIK

We try to get the girls to come but they think it's pretty lame, you know?

DEIRDRE

Yeah, we know it's cheesy but we like it 'cause they take care of everything, you feel taken care of . . .

RICHARD

Yeah, I get that. Are you able to avoid all of the touristy stuff when you dock? / Or do you—

DEIRDRE

All of the . . . well, they let you off in good spots usually . . . where there's a lot to do . . . ?

RICHARD

Oh, cool . . .

DEIRDRE

. . . yeah . . .
(*small beat*)
. . . the spots are pretty good usually . . . where they leave you off at.

UPSTAIRS:
Brigid is still listening to this conversation. It makes her sad.

STEPHEN KARAM

RICHARD

Cool, cool . . . I tend to be more of a . . . I like to wander off the
beaten path . . .

DEIRDRE

No, I hear you . . . Brigid's the same way . . .

RICHARD

Can I [pour you more wine] . . . ?

DEIRDRE

Thanks . . .
 (beat)
There's usually decent entertainment options on the ship, lotta
the singers have professional credits. Lotta stuff going on all at
once . . .

<table>
<tr><td align="center">RICHARD</td><td align="center">ERIK</td></tr>
<tr><td>Sounds awesome.</td><td>Yeah, yeah, so at night she can go see a show and I can go, you know, go do / something else . . .</td></tr>
</table>

DEIRDRE

Gamble. You gamble.

ERIK

Or whatever else I feel / like doing . . .

DEIRDRE

Well c'mon, don't act like you play shuffleboard on the lido deck.

UPSTAIRS:
Brigid finally heads downstairs. Erik passes her, going upstairs.

BRIGID

Hey . . .

ERIK

 (to Brigid, ascending the stairs)
Just gonna check the score of the game . . .

Okay . . .

UPSTAIRS:	DOWNSTAIRS:
Erik climbs the stairs, struggles for reception by the window.	DEIRDRE *(pushing her Ensure shake closer)*
He sees some falling ashes. *It looks like light flurries.*	Mom, you're not hungry? Just finish drinking your—
Perhaps the smallest suggestion of a moving shadow in the alley.	*Momo overturns her Ensure shake, splattering it everywhere. She mumbles under the following:*
Erik's a bit unsettled by what he sees, he steps away from the window, takes a few calming deep breaths . . .	MOMO Sorn it all / . . . sorn it all sezzor dollen black? Homeran sinitz inner therell . . . sornitz allinners . . . sorn it allinners . . .

DEIRDRE
Oh man . . . I got it, you're all right, Mom . . .
 (calling up)
Erik . . .

BRIGID
Mom, let him go, I got it—we have loads of paper towels . . .

RICHARD
Where are they?

BRIGID	MOMO
They're in the shopping bag upstairs, Rich, can you— I got it, Mom . . .	*(tapering to calm and quiet)* . . . sinnin . . . sahn . . . airywheres . . . itsen . . . senna . . .

DOWNSTAIRS:

Brigid cleans up the mess, back and forth between the kitchen, soaking up the liquid and ringing out her kitchen towel in the sink, while Deirdre wheels Momo away from the mess and into the other downstairs room, calming her.

UPSTAIRS:

Richard arrives upstairs, passes Erik.

<table>
<tr><td align="center">RICHARD</td><td align="center">MOMO</td></tr>
<tr><td align="center">*(passing Erik)*</td><td align="center">*(tapering to quiet)*</td></tr>
<tr><td>We had a minor spill . . .</td><td>. . . sinnin . . . sahn . . . airy-
wheres . . . itsen . . . senna . . .
sahn . . . airywheres . . . itsen
. . . senna . . .</td></tr>
</table>

DEIRDRE

(to Momo)
There you go . . .

Richard gets the paper towels in the next room. He comes back toward the stairs, stops, seeing Erik is still staring out the window.

RICHARD

. . . you okay?

ERIK

Uh, yeah, just worried about the roads. It's snowing out there . . .

RICHARD

(looking out the window)
Oh. No, I think someone from a higher floor just emptied their ashtray.

DOWNSTAIRS:

Deirdre has been helping Momo up and onto the couch.

DEIRDRE

There we go . . . / there we go . . .

ERIK

Hey make sure you get blinds up, will you? You don't want people looking in on you . . .

RICHARD

Yeah, no I'm on it, this week I'll put some up.

Richard descends the staircase with the paper towels.

DEIRDRE

You feeling good, Mom? . . . now you can rest . . . there you
go . . .

UPSTAIRS:	DEIRDRE
Aimee exits the bathroom,	*(seeing Richard clean up*
phone in hand. A bit nervous,	*the last of the spill)*
she makes a call. She doesn't	Thanks, Rich . . . we got
know Erik is in the next room.	most of it . . .

RICHARD

Okay, no problem . . .

DOWNSTAIRS:

*Richard heads to the kitchen. Brigid's back is to us, her hands
on the sink counter. She rings out the towel, appears to be de-
stressing, taking a moment for herself.*

AIMEE

(on her cell)
Hey, hi . . . Happy—I know—Happy Thanksgiving—
I know, but—
I know, I know . . .

BRIGID

Ahhh . . . [will we make it through dinner?]

RICHARD

Can I get you anything?   AIMEE

                    uh-huh . . .

BRIGID	AIMEE
Can I get *you* anything?	
	. . . mm-hm . . .

Richard kisses her, she smiles, he pulls her farther into the kitchen alley . . .

UPSTAIRS:
Aimee continues her phone conversation. In the next room, Erik listens.

AIMEE

I know, I know, I just thought the holidays could be an exception . . .
. . . uh-huh . . . well sorry if—
I understand, I just wanted to hear your—
no I get it, I get it . . .
I'm good, you know?, I'm okay . . . and you're, are you upstate with the fam, or? . . .
(hurt, but not showing it)
. . . oh . . . no, I figured you were seeing someone . . . I saw your pics online—
no I think it's good . . . I've been dating too . . . so . . .
yeah, nothing serious, but . . .

AIMEE	BRIGID
. . . yeah, yeah . . .	*(calling from the kitchen)*
	Mom, does Momo need
	another shake?

DEIRDRE

Sure, let's give it a try . . .

Brigid gets a shake out of the fridge.

UPSTAIRS:
Erik moves in a bit closer, listening to Aimee's phone conversation.

STEPHEN KARAM

64

AIMEE
. . . well hey, I'll let you go, but glad you're—
. . . ha, I'll tell them, they'll appreciate that . . . so—
absolutely, and love to your—
exactly, Happy Thanksgiving and—
   (hurt, but trying to keep things light)
—well don't wish me a Merry Chr—
we can talk again before *Christmas* . . .

DEIRDRE	AIMEE
(laying Momo on the couch)	. . . uh-huh . . .
There you go . . . there you	
go . . .	
	. . . yeah . . .
Deirdre steps away from Momo	
to tell Brigid to forget the	
Ensure shake, and catches a	
glimpse of Richard and Brigid	. . . uh-huh . . .
enjoying a quiet moment—	
they're just visible in the kitchen	
alley. They are laughing about	. . . uh-huh . . .
something. Richard kisses her	
forehead, then slaps her on the	
ass playfully. Richard disappears	
into the alley as she slaps his ass	
back. This stirs something inside	
Deirdre. She retreats back to	
the couch.	

AIMEE
   (successfully fighting back tears)
. . . huh, uh-huh . . . well maybe your therapist is right . . .
. . . mm-hm . . .
. . . just, the holidays feel . . . *wrong*, without us at least—[talk-
ing] . . .
—no, I respect that . . .
. . . yeah . . . well look, love to all your—
. . . you too . . .
I will, I'll tell them . . .
okay, you too . . . bye . . .

Aimee hangs up. Erik knocks on the entryway.

ERIK

Hey . . .

Aimee cries, unable to hold it in. Erik holds her.

AIMEE

Ugh . . . I miss her . . .

ERIK

Hey . . .

AIMEE

. . . all the time . . .

ERIK

. . . we know . . .

DOWNSTAIRS:
*Brigid brings Deirdre and Momo a new Ensure shake with a
freshly rinsed straw. But Momo is now half-asleep.*

DEIRDRE

We'll try later, she's gonna sleep for a bit I bet . . .

*Deirdre adjusts Momo's head, maybe with a memory-foam travel
pillow they always take with them. Brigid returns the shake to
the kitchen. Richard abandons dinner preparations and emerges
from the kitchen alley with a bottle of wine.*

RICHARD	AIMEE
(regarding the wine)	Gimme a sec . . .
May I . . .	

DEIRDRE

Thanks, yeah . . .

BRIGID
I wish you knew her before
she got sick, Rich . . .

*Aimee breaks her embrace with
Erik.
She goes to the bathroom to
get some toilet paper to wipe
her nose/dry her tears.*

DEIRDRE
She was something, she refused
to quit driving, Rich, *refused*,
but . . . six years ago?, Erik
couldn't bring himself to take
the keys from her, so he got
her to take a driver's exam so
the decision wouldn't be on
him, and part of the test is— *Erik uses the moment alone*
they show her a picture of a *to wander down the hallway*
"yield" sign, but without the *and stretch out his lower back,*
word "yield" on it . . . well *which is bothering him.*
she can't name it, but enough
of her's still there that she
goes to the poor guy giving
the test, really pissed off,
she goes: "Trust me, I'd know
what to do if I was driving."
And he's like: "Then just tell *He eventually is drawn back*
me what you'd do if you were *to the window, inspects the*
driving and pulled up to this *alley. He stares out the window,*
sign." And she goes: "I'd see *rubbing his lower back.*
what everyone else was doing;
then I'd do that."

Richard smiles.

BRIGID
Where're you at with the whole . . . nursing home discussion? . . .

DEIRDRE
Mom's—as long as Uncle John can watch her weekdays, we're
fine—

BRIGID	RICHARD
I want you guys to [take care of yourselves]—	I love that—oh . . . I was just gonna say I love that you and Erik both call her "Mom."

DEIRDRE

Well, that's what she is to me, that's what's special about marriage, Rich, *real* marriage . . . you get two families.

BRIGID

("Give it a rest, Mom . . .")
Okay . . .

RICHARD

I'm very committed to Brigid.

UPSTAIRS:
Aimee exits the bathroom, spies Erik rubbing his lower back.

AIMEE

Hey . . .

DEIRDRE

I'm glad, that's good . . .

AIMEE

Big Guy, how's your back? . . .

ERIK

How's my back?, how's *your* back?

AIMEE

[That's a great point, Dad], you doing your exercises?

ERIK

Yeah, yeah . . .

DOWNSTAIRS:
Momo dozes off on the couch.

So it's okay if she sleeps here?

ERIK

You'll find someone new . . .

DEIRDRE

Oh yeah, the meds she's on—she gets in three good naps a day . . .

Deirdre helps adjust Momo on the couch. Brigid goes in search of the blanket.

ERIK

I mean it, hey, I'm serious, you're gonna find someone new—

AIMEE

Not with *history*—Carol knew me with *acne* . . . she helped me with my law school application . . .

ERIK

You're gonna come outta this stronger, / I promise.

AIMEE

Stop, Dad, stop lying to me.
    (beat)
Don't *actually* stop keep saying things to me . . .

DEIRDRE

Where's her blanket?

ERIK

Whattya want me to . . . Momo'd . . . if I skinned my knee or had any kinda setback, Momo'd say . . . "This, too, shall pass," / and I'd roll my eyes at her, but . . . this'll pass, it will . . .

BRIGID

Here . . .

DEIRDRE

Thanks . . . there we go . . .

RICHARD	AIMEE
(to Brigid)	Ugh . . . I need some more . . .
So turkey's out . . . I won't	bathroom time, I'll be down,
carve until we're all down	okay?
here, yeah?	

ERIK

Yeah . . .

BRIGID

(calling upstairs)
Dad! Aimee!

UPSTAIRS:
Aimee returns to the bathroom. Erik heads for the stairs.

DEIRDRE
(lovingly setting up Momo on the couch)
She's calm now, Rich, but . . . man—when she has a fit, it's like
watching her turn into someone else, you know? . . .

RICHARD
Can I help you get her [situated] . . . ?—

DEIRDRE
Yeah, just, lift her feet there . . .

*Richard moves her feet into a more comfortable position. Erik is
on his way downstairs.*

ERIK
Hey, get your hands off of my mother, / you bastard!—

RICHARD	BRIGID
Oh my God I was just—	Dad—stop—
	(to Richard)
	—he's teasing you . . .

ERIK

(smiling)
The Lions are up ten.

BRIGID

Your sense of humor is terrible.

DEIRDRE

Have you guys noticed that *everyone's* sense of humor is terrible except for Brigid's? / How interesting . . .

ERIK   RICHARD

Score one for Mom!   Amen, yes . . .

DEIRDRE   BRIGID

How's Aimee?   Not funny.

ERIK

Give her five minutes, she's okay . . .
    (Deirdre isn't convinced)
. . . she's okay . . .

DEIRDRE

I was telling Rich, before we got her on these new meds . . . you coulda put some of her worst outbursts in a horror flick.

ERIK

Brigid's? / I agree . . .

BRIGID

Dad!

Richard finds this joke pretty funny. Brigid laughs, too.

DEIRDRE

. . . I'm serious, I keep seeing ads for that zombie show on TV . . . it's awful, but it makes me think of / Mom's worst [tantrums]—

ERIK

Yeah, but we're doing okay, right? We're okay . . .

DEIRDRE

Yeah, with the help of God, yeah . . .

(small beat)

. . . [I] can't believe people wanna watch that stuff at night /
when there's—

BRIGID

She hates anything with blood or gore—

DEIRDRE

—yeah, well there's enough going on in the real world to give
me the creeps, / I don't need any more . . .

RICHARD

That's like—I bet she'd appreciate—there's this comic book
called *Quasar* . . . I was obsessed with it as a kid, / it's about this—

BRIGID

You're *still* obsessed with / *Quasar*, he won't throw them out . . .

RICHARD

Yes I am, be quiet—it's about this species of like half-alien,
half-demon creatures with teeth on their backs—

BRIGID	RICHARD
Oh my God . . . just call them monsters—	—but on their planet—

RICHARD

—on their planet, the scary stories they tell each other . . .
they're all about us. The horror stories for the monsters are all
about humans. / I love that . . .

BRIGID	DEIRDRE
(joking, to Erik)	(to Richard)
Thank God he's in grad school . . .	Yeah well people are [terrifying] . . . you should meet my boss . . . no teeth on his back, but man . . .

But monsters aren't *scared* of us, / so why would—

Sure they are, it's always a man driving a stake through the heart of the vampire—or if you're a zombie, you eat people but your biggest threat is what?—getting killed by an enterprising human, / right?

I get it, Rich . . .

They'd be more scared by monster-eating monsters or something, am I right?

Monsters aren't real so it's a weird thing to wanna be right about.

RICHARD	DEIRDRE
That's probably the soundest	Yeah . . . well . . . that's not what you thought last night . . . you thought *that* was pretty real . . . there's sweat on the sheets to prove it . . .

(*smiling*)
Wow, you can't let that go, / can you?

Well tell me what you dreamed / and I'll drop it . . .

Well you're assuming I saw something specific when she was just / —it wasn't like that, okay?

BRIGID

Wait wait "she"?—so you *do* remember something specific /
about your dream—

ERIK	**DEIRDRE**
Oh man, you guys're relentless	Erik, have you been dreaming about a supermodel this whole time?—

Rich, help me out here . . .

RICHARD

(teasing)
Sorry, man, I tell Brigid my dreams all the time . . .

BRIGID

Yes you do, / all of them . . .

RICHARD	**BRIGID**
—two weeks ago, I dreamt my oldest sister was a mannequin working in a grocery store . . . what, I'm serious . . .	. . . Richard . . .

ERIK	**DEIRDRE**
All I remember . . .	Was yours that [weird]?— oh . . . what . . . ?

ERIK

. . . there's not much to . . .

BRIGID

Tell us . . . come on, Big Guy . . .

ERIK

. . . a coupla nights I've had this [recurring dream] . . .
. . . there'll be a, a woman . . .

BRIGID

Uh-huh . . . and . . .

(trying to remember)
. . . her back's to me . . . or maybe . . .
. . . something happens where . . .
. . . her head turns, and
I can see that her face is all . . . [messed up]

DEIRDRE   BRIGID
What?   Just tell us—

ERIK
. . . her skin's stretched over her eyes and her mouth . . .

BRIGID
Ewww . . .

DEIRDRE
She's got no face?

ERIK
. . . just skin where her eyes and mouth should be, / you know—

BRIGID
Ewwwww—

ERIK
—yeah, over the holes in her ears—

A THUD from above. Everyone jumps—

ERIK
Whoa, / whoa, how's that for timing? What the hell is going on
up there? . . .

BRIGID   RICHARD
Guys, sorry about that—   Okay, okay . . . yeah, maybe
                                   we *should* go up and say
                                   something . . .

BRIGID	DEIRDRE
Welcome to New York . . .	What do you think she's—is she exercising up there, do you think? . . .

ERIK

No, you think she's sweating to the oldies up there? / No way . . .

DEIRDRE

Oh wait, you know what it probably is? / I'm just realizing . . .

BRIGID	RICHARD
What is it?	What?

DEIRDRE

. . . it's the faceless lady, telling us to be quiet . . . / or maybe she wants some turkey . . .

ERIK	BRIGID
Nice . . . very funny . . .	Mom, are you drunk? . . .

In fact everyone has had just enough to drink that this starts to feel very funny.

DEIRDRE

(*fighting back laughter*)
—but how would she eat the turkey? She's got no mouth . . .

Deirdre mimes a woman without a mouth trying to eat turkey. It's so unfunny it's kind of funny. Eventually even Brigid laughs.

ERIK	BRIGID
I'm so glad I shared my nightmare, thank you for your love and support—	Oh my God, *stop* . . . Tell us the rest . . .

DEIRDRE

We're teasing!

RICHARD

Tough crowd, Erik . . .

BRIGID

Finish telling us your—

ERIK

Oh right, like I'm gonna— / you had your chance—yeah *now* you're sorry . . . man, you see what I'm up against, Rich?

DEIRDRE

I'm sorry, I'm sorry . . . oh don't punish us I'm just being silly, I'm sorry . . . how does it end?

UPSTAIRS:

Aimee calls from the top of the stairs.

AIMEE

Should I ask the dinosaur upstairs to tread a little more softly?

BRIGID

Not unless you speak Cantonese . . . / just come down . . .

RICHARD

Erik you'll appreciate this . . . last week I dreamed I fell through an ice-cream cone made of grass and became a baby.

BRIGID

Okay, no no no, save your dreams for Christmas, we're almost ready to eat here . . .
  (*calling up*)
. . . Aimee! . . .

UPSTAIRS:

From the apartment above them, the sound of running footsteps moving from one side of the room to the other. Aimee looks up. So does Erik. It's a bizarre noise—maybe the kind a tantrum-throwing toddler would make stomping about.

ERIK

Why don't I go up and ask her to just please / —just to please keep it down—

STEPHEN KARAM

BRIGID

No, no these floors are so old, Dad—hey, sit down . . .

Brigid runs up the stairs.

RICHARD

The whole building groans at times . . . we have two sets of ear plugs.

UPSTAIRS:

Aimee is responding to an e-mail on her phone. Brigid starts stomping around.

AIMEE

What are you doing?

BRIGID

Showing Dad how creeky the floors are . . .

ERIK

Okay . . . you don't have to do that!

Aimee starts jumping around with her. At a certain point the jumping and stomping become more about Aimee and Brigid releasing a lot of stress.

DEIRDRE

These floors are made of tissue paper . . .

RICHARD

Okay, honey, point proven!

They recover. Brigid playfully collapses on the floor, a bit exhausted. Aimee moves closer to the window for reception.

AIMEE

(*to her blackberry, referring to a new message*)
Stop e-mailing me . . .

DOWNSTAIRS:

RICHARD

Water and soda for dinner?

ERIK

Both—for the both of us, yeah?

DEIRDRE

Yeah, thanks . . .

BRIGID

(this has been on her
mind)

Did you see the Mary statue?
. . . and she's bringing up
marriage . . . we've been
doing so good, I dunno
why she's back to—

Richard is in the kitchen.

Deirdre checks in with Erik
about something; Erik nods,
then wanders into the adjoin-
ing room and paces.

AIMEE

(half-engaged with her
e-mail)

Being here's just . . . making
it more *real* for her, no?

Deirdre decides to give Erik
his space; she moves into the
kitchen to help Richard.

BRIGID

No, I dunno, something's
[not right] . . . I dunno . . .

AIMEE

(putting her blackberry
away)

. . . sorry—they even find
me on holidays . . . it never
ends . . .

. . . how's work for *you*? . . .

DEIRDRE

How can I help, Rich?

RICHARD

Uh, how about . . .

Uh, the restaurant pays me under the table so I can still collect unemployment, so that's been good . . . but . . . my *career* is . . . [nonexistent] . . . [I don't wanna talk about it] . . .

AIMEE

Hey, okay . . .

Brigid takes a deep breath, exhales.

BRIGID

I'm just glad Rich and I made the leap, / it was time, you know?

AIMEE   DOWNSTAIRS:

Yeah . . . he's great, Bridge . . .

BRIGID   *Deirdre continues to help*
Yeah, we were always at each   *Richard in the kitchen. They*
other's place, so financially it *are occasionally half heard*
was just stupid, you know . . .   *speaking to each other. Erik*
Rich made up this list of pros   *is the prominent figure down-*
and cons . . . to move in or   *stairs—he paces in the hall,*
not to move in . . . Aimee,   *refers to a piece of paper.*
his *lists* . . . I found one posted
to the fridge last week called:
"ways to have fun"; [What
the fuck?!]—stuff like: dance
with yourself; take long walks
at sunset . . . game nights . . .

AIMEE

That's endearing . . .

BRIGID

I know . . .

Audible-but-indecipherable conversation between Deirdre and Richard in the kitchen alley.

BRIGID

I dunno, we were happy without making it so official, so / . . .
I dunno . . .

AIMEE

Yeah, well . . . Carol and I broke up because . . . we were unhappy?
. . . and now I'm [wondering] . . .
maybe loving someone long-term is more about . . .
deciding whether to go through life unhappy alone . . .
or unhappy with someone else?

BRIGID

Richard can draw up a list of reasons why your breakup was a
good thing, if you want . . . / I can ask him to draft a very long
list—

AIMEE

No, shuttup so . . . ugh: I need to have that surgery . . . / the
one where they'll—

BRIGID

What? I thought you could put that off until your sixties or—

AIMEE

This test showed—it's just dysplasia which means . . . it's not
cancer, but with colitis it'll become cancer if they don't take it
out, so . . .

BRIGID

You'll lose the whole intestine?

AIMEE

It cures the disease, though, so . . . but . . . yeah . . . they make
a hole in your abdomen so the waste can, you know . . .

BRIGID

Do Mom and Dad know?

AIMEE

No, I don't want to discuss it at dinner and . . . I'm okay, I'm mostly just like . . . uhhhh, how am I gonna find another girl-friend? . . . / I'm serious . . .

BRIGID

You're a complete catch.

AIMEE

I'm gonna be pooing out of a hole in my abdomen. Who's gonna date me?

BRIGID

Lots of people . . .

AIMEE

Lotta *ugly* people . . .

BRIGID

Aimee!

AIMEE

. . . lotta troll ladies, who'll have their own troll problems . . .

BRIGID

Stop . . .

AIMEE

. . . living under bridges . . .

BRIGID

. . . if you shat out your ears—if they re-routed your colon to your *ears* I'd still marry you.

AIMEE

Uh-huh . . . when do I even—do I wait until the third date to be like: "Just FYI, I shit out of a hole in my belly." Is that a fifth date thing?

BRIGID

Sorry you have to go through all that.

Audible-but-indecipherable talk between Richard and Deirdre in the kitchen alley.

Erik resolves to go upstairs, but stops near the top of the staircase when he realizes the girls are talking about him.

> AIMEE
>
> I'm more worried about—did you notice Mom's knees? . . . Going down / the stairs . . .

> BRIGID
>
> I saw, yeah . . . I'm afraid to ask how her arthritis is . . . or Dad's back . . . / I don't wanna know . . .

> AIMEE
>
> Well it's bothering him—can't you tell he's—

> BRIGID
>
> No, yeah, do you think it's because . . . he hasn't been sleeping, right? . . .

The light fixture above them burns out.

BRIGID	AIMEE
Shit . . .	Was that the light?

DOWNSTAIRS:
Erik shifts his direction and heads back downstairs, hurt by what he's overheard.

> DEIRDRE
>
> What are they doing up there?—

ERIK	BRIGID
They're coming, they're coming . . .	*(calling down)*
(aside, to Deirdre)	Richard . . . Rich . . . babe, do we have a spare bulb? The
I'll talk to them after dinner . . .	light up here is out.
I'll talk to them later . . .	

RICHARD

(*calling up*)
Can you just . . . open the bathroom door, let that light spill
into—

BRIGID

Richard, that's not a very good solution to the problem—

RICHARD

Well, I'm not a magician, do you want me / to make a light bulb
appear out of thin air?

DEIRDRE

Well hey, how—Rich . . . how 'bout, there's an LED lantern in
our care-package . . . lemme get that out so it's not like a cave
up there . . . problem solved . . .

RICHARD

Uh, sure . . . thanks, Deirdre.

Deirdre goes upstairs.
Brigid turns on the light in the bathroom and opens the door;
Aimee opens the care-package box.

BRIGID

You bought us a *lantern?*

ERIK

(*calling up*)
I bought it. After what the hurricane did to this neighborhood
. . . you can't be without light, not in a basement apartment.
They say another storm's gonna strike this year . . . you're in a
Zone A flood zone.

DOWNSTAIRS:
Richard takes care of final table arrangements.

UPSTAIRS:
Deirdre and Aimee and Brigid sift through her care-package box.

AIMEE

Cans of tuna? Oh Mom . . .

DEIRDRE

You gotta be prepared . . .

RICHARD

I don't blame you for worrying, especially after—Brigid told me about . . . you and Aimee.

ERIK

Yeah, well . . .

UPSTAIRS:

BRIGID

There are literally three thousand double-A batteries in here.

. . . yeah . . .

DEIRDRE

There are literally twelve.

. . . what's funny is Bridge is the one who'd been—you can imagine her as a teenager, she was a piece of work, she loved teasing me because Scranton's a stone's throw from the greatest city in the world but I've never even, you know, I'd never seen the Statue of Liberty, never seen the . . . [anyway . . .]

Deirdre puts batteries into two flashlights and the lantern. Aimee heads to the window to deal with work e-mails.

. . . she's a piece of work . . . [anyway] . . .

BRIGID

A wind-up radio?

. . . so when—
Aimee got a, an interview to be a paralegal at this New York firm . . . I took the day off, drove her in . . . Aimee's at her interview by 8:45, thirty-

DEIRDRE

You'll thank me later.

THE HUMANS

ERIK

seventh floor and . . . I'm at a Dunkin' Donuts across the street 'cause the observation deck didn't open until 9:30, / otherwise . . .

RICHARD

Oh man . . .

BRIGID

(to Aimee)
Stop checking your e-mail.

ERIK

. . . yeah, took me hours to find her 'cause . . . I had no cell then . . . but . . .

RICHARD

Man, I can't even [imagine] . . . / it's just crazy . . .

ERIK

. . . yeah . . . well . . . what's crazy is how you still mess up . . .
it's crazy how you you still—

DEIRDRE

(Turning on the lantern)
There we go . . .

Deirdre walks into the darkest spot in the upstairs hallway to place the lantern on the floor. Brigid is about to head back downstairs . . .

UPSTAIRS:
Deirdre screams. Her lantern falls to the floor.

ERIK	**RICHARD**
What? / What's wrong?	Hey you okay?

DEIRDRE

It was a rat or something . . . oh God . . . where did it go? / Did you see it?

Brigid shines her flashlight on the floor. Erik and Richard arrive upstairs.

STEPHEN KARAM

86

ERIK	AIMEE
What's wrong you okay? /	Oh my God I absolutely saw
What happened?	that what was that?!?

BRIGID	RICHARD
Okay don't scream—American	Okay, okay, I'll get it . . .
cockroaches are huge . . . I'm	
sure it was just a cockroach—	

DEIRDRE

I have nothing to stand on . . . someone give me something to
stand on . . .

BRIGID

It was an American cockroach, they're huge / okay?—don't get
so upset—

AIMEE

Ewwwww . . .

DEIRDRE

A cockroach the size of a mouse *is* upsetting!

DOWNSTAIRS:

*Momo wakes up, stumbles off the couch, slowly plods to the
kitchen . . .*

AIMEE	DEIRDRE
Ahhhh, I can't be up here	Shouldn't we kill it?
right now . . . no, Mom,	
c'mon . . .	

BRIGID	RICHARD
I'm not killing it . . .	*(laughing)*
	I'll get it if it comes back . . .

DEIRDRE

(laughing)
Don't laugh at me . . .

The cockroach-melee winds down. Erik heads back downstairs.

ERIK	BRIGID
(to Richard)	Okay, okay . . . everyone retreat
You gotta caulk. If you let	. . . it's just a cockroach . . .
me caulk and put down	
some boric acid . . .	

RICHARD	DEIRDRE
I hear you, Erik, I will . . .	Jesus, Mary and Joseph . . .
okay, everyone down for	
dinner, sorry for the bug	
scare . . .	

Erik descends the stairs and doesn't see Momo.

AIMEE
(to Brigid)
I had roaches in my first Philly apartment . . .

DEIRDRE
I should have included insect traps in the care-package—

ERIK
Mom . . . Mom . . . ? Hey where's . . . Dee, where's Mom? . . .

Erik checks outside the basement door; no sign of Momo.

ERIK	DEIRDRE
. . . help me look for her!	Well where could she—you
Just look!	want me to look under the
	couch where the hell could
	she be?!

A CRASH of a few empty pots and pans, maybe some knocked dishes, sounds from the kitchen alley. Erik disappears into the kitchen alley. Momo mumbles under the following scene as everyone tries to recover and Erik helps her back to the couch.

ERIK	MOMO
(offstage)	(offstage)
. . . Mom . . . / Jesus Christ . . .	. . . nairywheres do we blag werstrus, doll sezzer big sussten back . . . sezz it whairidoll . . . er hairin sildern fernal garn ackening ery or loddinsezz . . .

DEIRDRE	AIMEE
Is she okay?	What? Is she hurt?

ERIK	
(offstage)	BRIGID
. . . Jesus Christ . . . yeah, God . . .	What happened? Is she okay?

Erik returns, guiding Momo back to her wheelchair. Deirdre helps. Momo is fine.

ERIK

. . . yeah, she's okay, she almost burnt herself on the stove, God . . .

DEIRDRE

You were more scared than she was, you okay? / You're okay, Mom . . .

ERIK

Yeah, I shouldn't have left her . . .

AIMEE

She's okay / . . . I'll clean up in here . . .

BRIGID	ERIK
You okay, Big Guy?	I know, I know . . . yeah, I'm all right . . .

DEIRDRE	RICHARD
Why don't we give her her other pill before we eat . . .	I'll take care of the kitchen . . .

It's just some pots and pans, Dad, no worries . . .

Deirdre helps Erik with Momo. Erik gives her a pill.

RICHARD

We definitely owe you guys for that care-package, clearly we needed it.

ERIK

Yeah, you did, and cell-phone flashlights don't last long in a blackout. You gotta be prepared . . .

ERIK	AIMEE
. . . and I still don't get how you can live here after— *(to Aimee)* —or that it hasn't sent you back to church— / don't you think surviving that day means *something?*	Cut them a break, Dad—

AIMEE

Because for me—hey—hey—hey, I'm telling you what I think, I think it means the two of us were in New York on a terrible morning. / That's all . . .

ERIK

That's it?

AIMEE	BRIGID
Yes, Dad, that's it.	Yeah, me too—I'm not scared of coincidences—

DEIRDRE

Me too, they're not scary if you believe in some kinda God, / God doesn't make mistakes . . .

BRIGID

That, yeah, that wasn't my point, Sneaky—

All right, Momo's okay, yeah? / . . . that's what matters . . .

DEIRDRE	ERIK
Thank God, yes . . .	Yeah, man, you gave me a scare, Mom, / you really did . . .

Erik kisses Momo.

BRIGID

So, should—should we bring her wheelchair to the table for dinner?

DEIRDRE

No, no she'll be sleeping soon . . .

BRIGID

Does the medicine make her sleep?—should you be—

ERIK

It just calms her down—we can bring her to the table, / see how she feels—

BRIGID

Yeah, don't knock her out / just because—

DEIRDRE

Hey, if you want to come home more and help control her tantrums then you can judge the way we care for her.

BRIGID

I'm not trying to judge you I just want—can't you hire someone / to help with—?

DEIRDRE

It'd cost a hundred bucks a night to hire someone to watch her, *a hundred bucks* to make sure she doesn't / fall and get hurt—

ERIK

Hey . . . okay—

DEIRDRE

No, she needs to think before she opens her mouth.

BRIGID

Sorry.

Erik attends to Momo. Brigid focuses her energy in the kitchen.

AIMEE
(half-volume, to Deirdre)
Let's all just . . . [calm
down] . . .

. . . God bless us, everyone . . .

DEIRDRE
Yeah, yeah . . .

BRIGID
Do we need anything else, Rich?

RICHARD
No we're good, babe . . . you
okay?

BRIGID
Yeah . . . how's the turkey?

RICHARD

It's great—will everybody eat dark meat? / Or just—

AIMEE

We'll eat it all, Rich, / just send it our way . . .

ERIK

(this is a funny question)
Will we eat dark meat?

DEIRDRE

Yeah but—I will, I'm just . . . oh man, I'm just . . . I'm back on
Weight Watchers / and man . . .

AIMEE

That's great, Mom . . .

DEIRDRE

. . . thanks, yeah . . . it's tough, one baby ice-cream cone takes
up half my points for the day . . . same for a junior cheeseburger
at Wendy's, it's tough staying on track.

Especially if you eat a bucket of ranch dip before dinner.

AIMEE

[Don't say stuff like that . . .]

Richard returns from the kitchen area, sets down final side dishes. He isn't aware of how wounded Deirdre is at this moment. Erik is also unaware as he arrives at the table. Momo is awake but doesn't seem very alert.

DEIRDRE

(to Brigid)
I'm, uh, not being careful with points today, / not on holidays . . .

RICHARD

. . . this is the last side dish, yeah? Think we're good to go— / are we ready . . . ?

AIMEE

Uh-huh . . . / let's eat . . .

ERIK

(sitting down, gesturing for them to hold hands)
Okay . . . hands . . .

They bow their heads, hold hands for grace. Richard doesn't know the grace but participates in the hand-holding.

ERIK

Bless us oh Lord . . .

ERIK, AIMEE, BRIGID, DEIRDRE AND MOMO

. . . and these Thy gifts, which we are about to receive, from Thy bounty, through Christ our Lord, amen.

They have all noticed that Momo joined in. They smile, thrilled.

ERIK

Did you / hear that?

BRIGID	AIMEE
Momo, I'm so glad you're here!	Amazing . . .

ERIK

Is it crazy if we do it again? Just / one more time . . .

They all ad-lib "no" . . .

AIMEE

. . . no, go for it.

ERIK
(smiling, holding their hands again)
Bless us oh Lord . . .

Momo joins in again.

ERIK, AIMEE, BRIGID, DEIRDRE AND MOMO
. . . and these Thy gifts, which we are about to receive, from Thy bounty, through Christ our Lord, amen.

This time they all spontaneously clap, Momo does too. They laugh at their impulse to applaud an old woman for saying grace.

ERIK

Mom, you remember Aimee and Brigid, these are your grand-daughters . . .

Momo picks up the serving spoon in the sweet potatoes and is about to take a bite—Erik catches her in time, removes the serving spoon from her hand . . .

AIMEE	BRIGID
Don't put the spotlight on her . . .	We're happy you're here, Momes. Guys, dig in, don't wait . . .

They start to eat, pass the food around the table.

ERIK

Wow, all looks great.

Everyone ad-libs agreement.

DEIRDRE

This looks good, what's this . . .

BRIGID

It's a rainbow chard salad, it's packed with nutrients . . . everything else is familiar, I think . . .

DEIRDRE

You guys did a great job . . .

RICHARD	ERIK
Thanks.	Awesome.

They eat.

MOMO

Dig a hole shower.

They all laugh at the randomness of the remark.

ERIK

This is definitely not one of your better days, Mom . . . oh man,
we, uh . . . we'll all be there some day, right? . . . / We love you
so much, Mom . . .

AIMEE	RICHARD
Yes we will be . . .	Dig in, everybody, please . . .

They eat.

DEIRDRE

This turkey is so moist, / good job guys . . .

ERIK

Mm-hmm . . .

Shower in holes.

*They all stifle laughter, acknowledge the remark; it's funny, but
also a little upsetting.*
They eat.
Aimee starts laughing.

ERIK

What?

AIMEE

Momo's Christmas toast . . .

*They all start laughing. Richard doesn't know what this inside
joke is.*

BRIGID

On Christmas, Momo—she always delivers a traditional Irish
toast, it's ancient, right?

ERIK

It's ancient and it's beautiful, but one year Aimee's mind was
in the gutter—

AIMEE

I was twelve!

BRIGID

And ever since, the blessing sounds kinda dirty to us—

DEIRDRE   ERIK
Not to us . . .   To *you guys* it sounds dirty . . .

RICHARD

What's the blessing?

AIMEE

"May the Virgin and her Child lift your latch on Christmas
night."

Some wine dribbles out of Richard's mouth; he wasn't expecting to find it that funny.

<table>
<tr><td>DEIRDRE</td><td>AIMEE</td></tr>
<tr><td>Not you too, Rich . . .</td><td>I know, right?! They don't get it . . .</td></tr>
</table>

ERIK

We *get* it we just don't agree . . .

DEIRDRE

. . . I first thought latch-lifting was a kinda sexual position . . .

<table>
<tr><td>BRIGID</td><td>DEIRDRE</td></tr>
<tr><td>Ewww, Mom . . .</td><td>. . . I'm serious, thought maybe it was like scissoring, or / something—</td></tr>
</table>

BRIGID

Mom! / Eeewwww . . .

AIMEE

Oh my God, Mom, I'm never telling you anything again, /we're not discussing this at the table . . .

BRIGID

. . . you must never say the word "scissoring" again . . .

RICHARD

I'm steering clear of this conversation . . .

ERIK

(to Richard)
Its *real* meaning is beautiful—it's old Irish custom to leave the door unbolted and a candle in the window for Mary on her way to Bethlehem.

AIMEE

Well, it's premature, but . . . in honor of you, Momo . . .
(a toast, struggling not to laugh)
May the Virgin and her Child lift all of your latches . . .

They all ad-lib "cheers," "amen," "here here," etc. . . . Erik lovingly disapproves of Aimee's joke, notices Momo's a bit dazed, her neck is not at a comfortable angle.

ERIK

Okay, this isn't gonna [work]—she's gonna be dozing off soon, / lemme get her settled—

DEIRDRE

Want me to—

ERIK

—no I got it, I got it . . . keep eating guys . . .

Erik wheels Momo back to the couch, gets her settled there.

DEIRDRE

Where's your family, Rich? They upset we stole you away?

RICHARD

Oh, they're good, thanks. My dad's in L.A. and my mom's on the Cape now.

DEIRDRE

What cape?

BRIGID

Cape Horn, Mom—you know he's from / Massachusetts—

AIMEE

Hey, hey . . . it's not a dumb / question . . .

BRIGID

Cape *Cod*, sorry . . . I'm sorry.

Small beat.

DEIRDRE

What's your mom do, Rich?

RICHARD
She's a therapist . . . / she works from home . . . yeah . . .

DEIRDRE
Oh wow, that's great . . . do you guys have any Thanksgiving
traditions?

RICHARD
Uh, some, yeah, we usually start our morning off volunteering
at this soup kitchen about thirty minutes from our house, so . . .

DEIRDRE
That's beautiful, I volunteer with the Bhutanese now, / every
week they have—

BRIGID
Mom, we know.

RICHARD   AIMEE
No, I'm interested . . .   *(to Brigid)*
                                [Why are you being such a
                                bitch?]

DEIRDRE
They uh, the Bhutanese, the level of poverty, guys, is just . . .
[unimaginable] . . .

They eat. Erik returns to the table after getting Momo settled.

ERIK
(to Richard)
You balancing a job with all your studies . . . or just racking up
the college loans?

RICHARD
Ha, I've gone the loan route but I plan on paying them off as
soon as possible . . .

BRIGID
His grandmother—he's getting a small trust when he turns
forty—can I tell them?

RICHARD

You want to know if you can tell them *after* you tell them? /
Seriously?

DEIRDRE   AIMEE
Like a trust fund?   Pass the . . . / yeah, thanks . . .

BRIGID

Sorry—babe, sorry, don't be embarrassed . . .

RICHARD   BRIGID
I'm *not* embarrassed—   —it's actually great—his
                                 grandmother didn't want him
                                 spoiled so he doesn't see any of
                                 the money until he's forty.

ERIK

(*teasing*)
You haven't reached that milestone yet, Rich?

BRIGID   RICHARD
Ha, ha . . .   (*smiling*)
                                    No, not quite, I'm thirty-eight . . .

DEIRDRE

Having to wait until your forties is a—your grandma's a smart
lady, it's like that—'member that e-mail I forwarded you guys
about Andrew Carne—is it Ca*r*negie or Car*n*egie, / I never
remember . . .

RICHARD   ERIK
Pretty sure Car*n*egie is correct   Carnegie Hall, right? Ca*r*negie
. . . oh, maybe,yeah . . .   Hall . . .

DEIRDRE

I forwarded it, Rich, 'cause it had this great answer to the question: "What makes Americans powerful and influential and
wealthy?"

Small beat as they eat.

STEPHEN KARAM

Trust funds?

No . . . not trust funds, / smart-ass . . .

What—too soon? Too soon? . . .

Yes, too soon . . .

What makes a person powerful and influential and wealthy is *not* growing up with power and influence and wealth. That's what the e-mail said, anyway . . .
> *(caught off-guard by her emotions)*
. . . the gift of poverty is a . . . it's not a myth, / it's a real thing, it can be a blessing . . .

Whoa, Mom, are you okay?

Yeah I'm just happy to be with my girls, sorry . . .

They eat. Brigid mouths, "Get a grip . . ." to herself.
Erik cracks open another beer.

One thing I learned, Rich—and the older I get I see this—it's that having too much money—it can be just as bad for you as, you know, *not* having enough, / you know? Gotta be careful . . .

> *(embarrassed)*
Dad, why're you—what are you talking about—

I think I know what you're saying—do you mean—

THE HUMANS

ERIK

I'm saying—Dee's bosses have more money than God and they're stingy with her on everything, bonuses, vacation days . . . Aimes gets fired 'cause she's sick—*my* grandma almost lost her life in a fire 'cause her bosses locked the doors to her factory to keep 'em from taking breaks, coupla blocks from here, so—and this isn't some scientific notion or something—but, yeah, I do notice that rich people are usually pretty messed up.

BRIGID	AIMEE
[Oh God . . .]	That's an elegant thesis, Dad.

RICHARD

Well, no, no, it's a good point, I just don't think being messed up is *necessarily* linked to how much money is in your bank account.

BRIGID	ERIK
Of course . . .	Yeah, but it *can* shift your priorities in ways that aren't good.

RICHARD

We agree on that, yeah, but so can being poor. Right? / Just meaning—

BRIGID	AIMEE
Yes . . .	Everyone's right, guys . . .

RICHARD

—I actually agree with you, I'm just adding that . . . yes, wealth can ruin people but so can poverty.

DEIRDRE

Well I'd rather be ruined in a Four Seasons somewhere, on a beach, you know? . . . I'll take wealth for four hundred, Alex . . .

BRIGID	AIMEE
Mom, that doesn't even make sense . . .	Oh, Mom . . .

RICHARD

I hear you, I'm just proud that my family went out of their way to ensure—you *do* get that I'm not able to touch my money until I'm forty, right?

ERIK

Uh-huh, but do *you* get how that sounds to a man my age?

RICHARD

No I hear you, I hear you . . . / I do . . .

AIMEE

. . . pass the—thanks . . .

BRIGID

We got the veggies from this farmer's market on Essex . . .

DEIRDRE

They're delicious . . .

BRIGID

We're gonna try and keep our fridge stocked with them, start juicing for breakfast.

AIMEE

Cool . . .

RICHARD

You guys liking any of the super-foods?

BRIGID

(to Aimee)
Rich made up a *list* that I e-mailed to these guys . . .

DEIRDRE

I even, I bought blueberries last week . . . they're not cheap.

ERIK

You also bought blueberry doughnuts.

DEIRDRE

Yeah, and you had three of them, so don't / act like you're better than me please.

ERIK

I did, no, I did.

AIMEE

Sadly, doughnuts are cheaper, too, huh?

DEIRDRE

Yeah.

BRIGID

Not cheaper when you consider
how much heart disease costs
once you're hospitalized.

They eat.

ERIK

So what, uh, when forty comes along, what happens . . . do you
just, do you retire?

AIMEE

Dad . . .

BRIGID

No, he's studying to become a
social worker . . .

RICHARD

Yeah, the main reason I'm not done with school yet is, I've been
/ in and out—

BRIGID

He took time off—

RICHARD

—yeah, because for a while / I was—

BRIGID

You don't have to tell them . . .

RICHARD

—it's fine—in my early thirties—I was depressed for a bit, so—
I'm fine now, just took me a while to get up and running again,
but . . . I've been better for years, it's why I'm comfortable talking about it . . .

ERIK

You take medicine for that?

BRIGID

Dad, that's rude / to ask—

RICHARD   ERIK

It's okay.   Sorry, hey, sorry, just . . . in our
                                        family we don't, uh, we don't
                                        have that kinda depression.

AIMEE

Yeah, no we just have a lot of stoic sadness.

They eat.

ERIK

(to Richard)
Well . . . I'm sorry, if—

RICHARD

[It's fine.]

ERIK

. . . makes you wonder if—the kind of faith *we* grew up with . . .
it's not perfect but you take for granted what a, a, a kinda natural antidepressant it is . . .

AIMEE

No religion at the table—

DEIRDRE

Hey, my mouth is shut, you know / where I stand . . .

BRIGID

Mom . . . you brought a statue of the Virgin Mary into our
house— / how is your mouth shut?

ERIK

All right, okay . . . I didn't mean to get us . . . I was just saying it's funny you guys'll try—you put faith in, in juice-cleansing or / yoga but you won't try church—

BRIGID

I did *one* juice-cleanse . . . *one* . . .

<table>
<tr><td>

ERIK

—you eat chard to feel your best but you still—you said half your friends are in therapy, / *you* said that so I'm asking—

</td><td>

DEIRDRE

My mouth is shut . . .

</td></tr>
</table>

BRIGID

That's because—yeah, I was trying to get you to pay for *mine*—I still can't afford it—

ERIK

Well save some of the money you spend on organic juice and pay for it yourself—

BRIGID

Don't criticize me for caring about my mental health—

AIMEE

Okay . . .

ERIK

Well what about—Rich's mom is a therapist—why don't you get it from her?—

<table>
<tr><td>

DEIRDRE

Erik . . .

</td><td>

BRIGID

Yeah, Dad, I'll get therapy from my mother-in-law, that's an awesome idea.

</td></tr>
</table>

Small beat.

DEIRDRE

She's not your mother-in-law unless you get married—

Mom . . . [don't] . . .

BRIGID
Looking for work every day, it's depressing—

ERIK
Well you've still got the will to eat super-foods—if you're so miserable why're you trying to live forever?

Aimee smiles involuntarily.

BRIGID
Last week—I shouldn't even tell you—

ERIK	RICHARD
Tell us what?	I don't think you appreciate how hard she's been working . . .

BRIGID	RICHARD
Babe, you don't have to—	. . . she's been bartending at two places while applying for every possible artist grant or residency you can think of . . .
Babe—	*(to Brigid)*
	. . . tell them, you'll feel better . . .

ERIK	BRIGID
Tell us what?	He won't care . . .

DEIRDRE	RICHARD
Tell us . . .	You'll feel better . . .

ERIK
Of course I'll care.

RICHARD
Read it to him, you'll feel better.

Brigid gets out her phone, searches for something.

This one professor has been writing all of her recommendation letters for all these applications and—

BRIGID

Yeah 'cause there's only one that I felt close to at school, who actually knew who I was, so . . . I was gonna miss this one deadline so I called his office and . . . his assistant agreed to e-mail the rec letter directly to me . . .

Brigid hands her iPhone to Erik, who reads the PDF of the letter on her phone.

AIMEE

What's it say?

BRIGID

. . . at least now I know why I'm not even getting interviews for unpaid internships.

ERIK
    (reading)
What's the big deal?—he didn't praise you enough?

Pissed, Brigid grabs her phone.

BRIGID

Are you kidding me?
    (reading)
"Brigid is a talented musician and composer; she served as a TA in my music theory class her senior year and many of the students noted how approachable and helpful she was to them in navigating the course. Initially, I must confess, I found Brigid's compositions almost willfully opposed to specificity and urgency. In her senior year, however, she showed marked improvement. And while her orchestral pieces still do not have the range or originality of her contemporaries, she always dis-

plays technical proficiency and great verve." [What does that even mean?!] "Her hard work and positive attitude have made her an asset to the music department."

(*eyes watering*)

. . . why wouldn't he respect me enough to say he couldn't do it?

Richard comforts her.

ERIK

You can always work retail.

DEIRDRE	AIMEE
Don't / tease her, babe—	Dad—Bridge, he's a dick for writing this—

RICHARD	ERIK
It's not easy to bounce back from this kind of thing, Erik—	. . . oh c'mon, hey, Rich don't treat me like—she knows I believe in her!—are you so spoiled you can't see you're crying over something hard work can fix?—

BRIGID

Everyone whose opinion I value has read this—

ERIK

Your grandma grew up in a two-room cesspool and your tragedy is what—having to figure out how to get a new letter of recommendation? / Sorry if I—

BRIGID	DEIRDRE
It takes *years* to build relationships with—	She knows all this . . .

ERIK

—you're lucky to have a passion to pursue, if you don't care about it enough to push through this setback you should quit and do something else . . .

DEIRDRE	AIMEE
All right . . . we're sorry,	*(to Erik)*
Bridge, that guy's a jerk . . .	Wow, what is up with you today?

UPSTAIRS: '
The light above the staircase burns out. The only light upstairs now comes from the open bathroom door.

BRIGID	RICHARD
Shit, another bulb's out . . .	Oh great . . . welcome to New York, guys . . .

DEIRDRE

It's just a light bulb . . . we'll live . . .

Brigid goes in search of a spare bulb. Erik follows her.

ERIK
(to Brigid, who is still angry with him)
Hey, hey, I don't wanna see you bent outta shape over something you can fix. / The Blakes bounce back, that's what we do.

BRIGID
Thanks . . . . . . uh-huh, yeah . . . . . . thanks, Dad, I don't really need a lecture now . . . Rich—why didn't we ask the landlord to replace all the light bulbs before we moved in?

RICHARD
Because that's a crazy thing to ask for, babe, no one asks for that.

DEIRDRE	ERIK
(stifling laughter)	Well, they're all probably on
Yeah, no one asks for that /	their last legs . . .
. . . and even if you did, it	
wouldn't matter, 'cause . . .	

AIMEE

What are you laughing at?

DEIRDRE

. . . she's burning out the bulbs to get our attention . . .

BRIGID   AIMEE

What?   What—who is?

DEIRDRE

She-With-No-Face . . . / she strikes again!

ERIK   AIMEE

Now you got her started . . .   What's so funny? What?

BRIGID

Dad sees faceless women in his sleep . . .

DEIRDRE

(going upstairs, wobbly ghost wail)
. . . wooooooooo . . .

RICHARD

Tough crowd, Erik . . .

AIMEE   ERIK

Where are you going, Crazy   You're telling me . . .
Lady?

DEIRDRE

The bathroom . . .
    (using a flashlight)
. . . this is gonna be like spelunking just to go pee . . . woooooo . . .

Now they are all laughing, even Richard.

UPSTAIRS:
Deirdre proceeds to the bathroom.

AIMEE

Who is this headless person?

BRIGID

Faceless, she's got skin covering her eye sockets / and mouth—

AIMEE	ERIK
Ewwwww . . .	All right, ha ha . . .

Brigid, still miffed by Erik's tough love, goes to the kitchen area.

BRIGID

. . . yeah, and I hope she visits you tonight in your sleep and casts an evil spell / on you—

ERIK

Oh yeah, smart-ass?—

Erik stops Brigid and bear-hugs her, making her laugh involuntarily.

BRIGID	ERIK
Stop! Dad! Oh *now* you	You don't know how good you
wanna be compassionate?!	have it . . .
Stop! The eyeless sorceress	
has all my support . . .	

RICHARD

Last week I dreamed I fell into an ice-cream cone made of grass and became a baby.

BRIGID

Richard, / are you kidding me with the sharing . . .

RICHARD

What?—I can share it if I want / —I restarted my life . . .

BRIGID

You can, and I love you, but when you share dreams in front of my family I become a crazy / person—

AIMEE

Hey, why don't—all right, Lover-Of-All, come on, come with me, let's get rid of some of this . . .

You want help?

No, you're good, you're good . . .

Aimee and Brigid make way to the kitchen. Aimee is half heard saying, "C'mon, Princess, step into my office . . ." as they ad-lib their way into the kitchen, carrying dishes.

RICHARD
I got to re-boot my life, it was good . . .

ERIK
I dunno. Doing life twice sounds like the only thing worse than doing it once.

They drink. Audible-but-indecipherable conversation from Aimee and Brigid in the kitchen.

RICHARD
The cone was made out of grass from my backyard . . . ?

ERIK
(*smiling*)
Out of / your backyard? . . .

RICHARD
. . . my backyard? . . . like it got twisted into an ice-cream cone? . . . in my head it was so normal . . .

They drink. Audible-but-indecipherable conversation from Aimee and Brigid in the kitchen.

ERIK
In mine there was this one other weird thing I . . . [remember] . . .

RICHARD
In your dream?

ERIK
(*nodding*)
[Yeah] . . . I didn't bring it up with—
The girls already think I'm losing it, you know but—
the woman without a [face] . . .
she's trying to get me in this, like a tunnel?

RICHARD
Yeah? And what do you do?

ERIK
Uh . . . I don't move, I dunno . . .

Erik shrugs it off, not wanting it to seem like a big deal.
More audible-but-indecipherable conversation and laughs from
Aimee and Brigid in the kitchen.

RICHARD
What's going on in there?

BRIGID
(*offstage*)
None of your business!

They drink.

RICHARD
Tunnels are—in my class we got this list of primitive settings?—
tunnels and caves, forests, the sea . . . stuff so a part of us
it's . . . you know, two hundred thousand years ago . . . someone
might've . . . closed their eyes and . . . seen a similar kind of
[image] . . . ?

A mechanical RUMBLE sounds from behind the basement door.

RICHARD
Trash compactor.

They drink. The RUMBLE stops.

RICHARD

Get in it next time, the tunnel . . .

ERIK

(*lighthearted*)
Thanks, / I'll try that . . .

RICHARD

I'm serious, get in it next time—
tunnels can just be,
stuff hidden from yourself?
so passing through one . . . [I dunno] . . . could be . . .
a favorable omen . . . you know?

ERIK

Is it a fortune-telling school you're at?

RICHARD

(*smiling*)
No . . .

ERIK

—"a favorable omen"?—

RICHARD

. . . no it is not . . .

ERIK

—you sure? You gonna bring out a crystal ball later?

CLANK *of pre-war pipes. The noise covers Deirdre opening the bathroom door.*
The girls return from the kitchen, laughing.

RICHARD

(*regarding their laughing*)
What?

AIMEE

We're conferring about . . . Mom's latest e-mail forward, / oh
man . . .

BRIGID	ERIK
(laughing)	Hey, hey shhhh . . .
Did you get it, Dad? . . .	

UPSTAIRS:

Deirdre stops in her tracks. We realize she can (most likely) hear their discussion.

AIMEE

(to Richard)

Rich, the subject line was: "PLEASE READ THIS" in all caps, all caps—so the e-mail got flagged by my IT department for being "potentially harmful" . . .

BRIGID

[Yeah], which was kinda prophetic.

RICHARD

Why—what did it say?

BRIGID

She forwarded a *Scientific American* article about how . . . nothing's solid; when you're touching a table, you're really feeling its molecules bouncing against—*we're* not even solid, we're, what . . . electrons / pushing back against everything . . . ?

AIMEE

Electrons, yeah . . . it also had vague religious overtones, there was a poem at the bottom in about ten fonts about how we already *are* a part of everything, how—

ERIK

Hey don't make fun of your mom, / no, I'm serious—

AIMEE	BRIGID
Dad, come on, it was a *little* crazy—	We're making fun of the e-mail . . .

AIMEE

—it was like: "Happy Tuesday, oh and just FYI: at the subatomic level, everything is chaotic and unstable . . . love, Mom."

ERIK

You have to start writing her back, okay? / I mean it . . . even to stuff like that . . .

AIMEE

You're right.

BRIGID

I know, I will . . .

So they won't know she's been listening, Deirdre walks to the bathroom door and shuts it again. Downstairs, they acknowledge the door shutting.

ERIK

. . . Rich, I hope you don't think the Blakes're [insensitive] . . . we're better than that, / we're drinking a bit too much here . . .

RICHARD

No, no way . . . and hey . . . no . . . if my family's meals *are* any calmer it's only because, the joke in my family is that our holidays are all sponsored by Klonopin, so / . . . or so the joke goes . . .

BRIGID

He doesn't think that . . .

ERIK

What's that?

Richard . . .

AIMEE

Just, it's medicine . . .

RICHARD

. . . sorry, [bad joke] . . .

Deirdre is now descending the staircase. Momo moans a bit in her sleep.

MOMO

(mumbled)

. . . you can never come black . . . / you can never come back you can never come back you can never come back you can never come back . . .

THE HUMANS

DEIRDRE
(*to Erik, checking on Momo*)
I got it, stay down . . .

Laundry-room noise sounds from behind the basement door.

BRIGID
That's the laundry room. That'll die down . . .

DEIRDRE
What kind of people would do laundry on Thanksgiving?

BRIGID
Mom, Chinese people.

The laundry-room noise dies down.

BRIGID
Having all this space makes it worth it . . . putting up with the noise.

AIMEE
(*clearing plates*)
. . . you done, Mom?

DEIRDRE
(*tending to Momo*)
Yeah, I'm full . . .

ERIK
The, uh . . . I should say the other thing I was . . . wanted to, uh . . . whoa . . . man, I haven't had that much to drink but my thought train just got all—

AIMEE
Your "thought train"? / Yeah I'd say your thought train just got derailed . . .

BRIGID
Stop drinking, then . . .

. . . I'm gonna have to call you a car, unless . . .

DEIRDRE
. . . Erik . . .

ERIK
No I'll stop drinking, I'm
done . . .

BRIGID
But unless you camp out here for a few more hours—

ERIK
Don't worry about me, I'm
fine—I was trying to
remember the pig-smash,
that's what I'm— / we're forgetting about our pig-smash . . .

AIMEE
You're too—Dad, grow up, I'm
calling you a car . . .

DEIRDRE
Okay, but . . . not sure we
[should until]—

BRIGID
Oh good idea, let's do it now . . .

RICHARD
Someone needs to explain the rules . . .

AIMEE
Mom, get over here, we're pig-smashing.

BRIGID
. . . we each pass it around, say what we're thankful for, then
we smash the pig . . .

AIMEE
And then we each eat a piece of the peppermint for good luck.

RICHARD
That is the weirdest tradition—

DEIRDRE
Please, *that's* the weirdest . . . ? Wait until you spend a Christmas with us . . .

She's threatening to invite all the Bhutanese in Scranton over for caroling.

DEIRDRE

Oh that's not a threat, honey, that's happening.

BRIGID

Here we go, why don't you start, babe.

RICHARD

Ah, now I'm nervous. Okay, uh . . .
. . . this year I'm most thankful for falling in love with Brigid . . .
and for . . . getting a new family in the process.
    (Awwws from everyone)
Now I . . . [smash the pig?] . . .

He takes the tiny mallet and smashes the pig.

BRIGID
    (with love)
That was a terrible smash . . . / do it harder . . .

RICHARD

Well I don't know . . . you made me go first!

BRIGID   AIMEE
Okay, Dad you go next . . .   Rich, it was a fine smash . . .

ERIK

Okay, well . . . I already gave one speech so lemme just say . . .
I'm thankful for having your unconditional love and support.
Hope there's nothing any of us could ever do to . . . change
that . . . what we've got right here, 'cause this is what matters . . .
this family . . .

He smashes the pig, passes the mallet to Deirdre.

DEIRDRE

All right, well I'm with your dad and—it may sound cliché, but
I'm thankful for the both of you . . .

Deirdre smashes the pig. She then hands the mallet to Brigid.

BRIGID

Okay . . . I'll state the obvious, there will never be a year I'm
not thankful that the observation deck didn't open until 9:30 . . .
so . . . and I'm grateful Momo's with us . . . oh—
   (to Erik)
—a wise old, haggard drunk man once told me that pursuing
your passion is a gift—so I'm grateful for that reminder . . . even
if I end up pursuing it while managing an H&M, / I'm lucky . . .
no I'm actually being serious about that, I am . . .

AIMEE	DEIRDRE
Ohhh so soon, so soon . . .	See what you've done?

BRIGID

(she's about to smash, then—)
And while everyone's [all here]—if anything were to ever hap-
pen to me, like an accident or whatever—and it won't, but: I'd
want to be cremated—I know it's weird to talk about but you
guys'd do open-casket so . . . I've been trying to find a way to
bring it up that isn't morbid or weird.

AIMEE

Well you didn't find it, Bridge.

Erik and Aimee are now laughing. Eventually Richard joins them.

DEIRDRE	BRIGID
Are you serious? You're crazy.	Oh come on—I *am* seri—
	. . . *You're* crazy . . . / no one
	in this family can handle
	honesty . . .

ERIK

You are a piece of work . . . God bless you, you are . . .

AIMEE

No you're right, Bridge, dinner is the perfect place to discuss
what we should do with your dead body . . . / thank you . . .

BRIGID

I hate you all.

AIMEE

. . . pass me that pig.
(*beat*)
All right. So. In a year where—I lost my job, my girlfriend, and
I'm bleeding internally . . . really a banner year . . . I'm thankful for what's *right*, okay? I *love* that in times like this I have
a home base, a family I can always come home to. Thanks for
giving us that.

BRIGID

You always have to win.

RICHARD

Yeah, she really *cremated* you.

Richard's joke is so lame it makes everyone laugh.

BRIGID

Wow just when you can't get / less funny . . .

DEIRDRE

(*laughing*)
She cremated you! She really cremated you . . . oh man . . .

They recover.

ERIK

How about for Momo—should we read Momo's e-mail?

BRIGID   AIMEE
Dad, no, it makes us cry—   Oh God . . .
                                     . . . get out the kleenex . . .

ERIK

This might be our last Thanksgiving together, can we please
give her a voice . . . ?

BRIGID	**AIMEE**
Of course . . .	Yeah, has he heard this?

RICHARD

I heard about it, but not the actual . . .

ERIK

She wrote this before she got really sick, Rich . . . an e-mail to these girls, what four years ago?

Erik finds the message on his phone.

DEIRDRE

Here, give it to me, you're gonna end up asking me to finish . . .

Erik hands her his phone.

DEIRDRE

"Dear Aimee and Brigid, I was clumsy around you both today and felt confused. I couldn't remember your names and felt bad about that. It's strange slowly becoming someone I don't know. But while I *am* still here, I want to say: don't worry about me once I drift off for good. I'm not scared. If anything, I wish I could've known that most of the stuff I *did* spend my life worrying about wasn't so bad. Maybe it's because this disease has me forgetting the worst stuff, but right now I'm feeling nothing about this life was worth getting so worked up about. Not even dancing at weddings."

(The Blakes smile. They have inside understanding of this remark)
"Dancing at weddings always scared the crap out of me, but now it doesn't seem like such a big deal. This is taking me forever to type. Consider this my fond farewell. *Erin go bragh.* Dance more than I did. Drink less than I did. Go to church. Be good to everyone you love. I love you more than you'll ever know."

They recover, some quiet tears of appreciation. They pass around the smashed pieces of peppermint; they each take a bite, one at a time.

RICHARD

I'm buying a pig for my family.

Richard starts to clear plates, goes to the kitchen.

BRIGID

(*to Erik*)
He wants you to like him.

DEIRDRE   AIMEE

We love him . . .   We do . . .

ERIK

Yeah, just look out for each other, okay?, that's what counts . . .

Erik goes to the kitchen for a beer.

DEIRDRE

Amen . . . in sickness and health / . . . for richer for poorer . . .

AIMEE

Tell that to Carol . . .
(*to Erik*)
Hey if you're having another beer, fine, but I'm calling a car for
you guys . . .

BRIGID   DEIRDRE

Thanks for drinking   Erik . . .
responsibly, Dad.

ERIK

I'm forgetting I'm not home, I'm sorry . . . I'm sorry . . .

AIMEE

I don't mind using my work account now that I'm on my way
out—

ERIK   DEIRDRE

No way, that's gonna cost a No way, no, I'll drive, I've been
fortune . . .   drinking water . . .

AIMEE   BRIGID

This is on me, it's not up for Mom for like the last ten
discussion—   minutes . . .

STEPHEN KARAM

124

No way, what'd we do about our car?

Aimee is already on her way upstairs.

AIMEE
I'm calling a car, / end of discussion.

BRIGID
Rich can drive it in tomorrow or—bus it into the city and help us paint this weekend, okay? We'll put you to work, just / take the car . . .

ERIK
Yeah, just, I'm not used to driving on Thanksgiving, Rich—

RICHARD
No worries—Bridge, should we re-park the car? I think it's street cleaning in the morning but . . . we'll figure it out . . .

Brigid mouths, "Thank you, I love you," into Richard's ear. They kiss. Their affection for each other triggers something in Erik— embarrassment that Richard needed to take care of him? Nostalgia for his own early romance with Deirdre?

The stage picture should subtly highlight Brigid and Richard's flawed-but-alive connection and a gulf between Erik and Deirdre. Erik decides to go upstairs.

Aimee has dialed her cell . . .

AIMEE
Hi I need a car . . . yeah, just charge it to my account . . . right, it's—zip is 18433 . . . Scott Township, Pennsylvania, . . . no case number, take it out of my personal . . . yeah, exactly . . . uh, three—but one of them is in a wheelchair—
    (to Erik, who has arrived upstairs)
Do you guys need a van for Momo . . . ?—

ERIK   DOWNSTAIRS:

Here, give it here . . . [mouths
"go downstairs" to Aimee]   *Richard and Brigid continue*
  (on the phone)   *bussing dishes; they set out a*
. . . hi, yeah three but . . . we   *dessert tray and some ice cream*
don't need a van it'll fit in the   *and spoons.*
trunk, it folds . . . uh-huh . . .
a lot cheaper or—? . . . then   *Deirdre—unseen by anyone—*
a van's good then that's fine   *is silently overcome with emotion,*
. . . uh-huh . . . yeah, uh-   *covers her face to stifle sobs.*
huh . . . *(wandering farther
back)* . . . can I use a credit
card for . . . yeah, but I'm
gonna be paying her back so
how much is—[wow, that's a
lot] . . . yeah . . .

*Erik wanders away from Aimee to finish the call with some
privacy. He finishes the call—including giving the car company
his cell phone number—with his back to us, he's audible-but-
indecipherable. Aimee rolls her eyes at Erik ordering the van.
She goes downstairs. Deirdre recovers from her crying spell when
she hears Aimee coming downstairs.*

RICHARD

Dessert is on the way . . .

AIMEE   DEIRDRE

Thank you . . . so is a car . . .   Oh man . . .
                                  . . . I can't believe there's more
                                  food . . .

Aimee helps bus some more dirty dishes to the kitchen.

AIMEE

(sensing Deirdre's a bit distressed)
Mom, don't worry about it, it saves me a cab ride—I can hitch
a ride with you guys to Penn Station . . .

ERIK

(*descending the stairs*)
Okay, they'll come at six . . . but we can change the time if you want . . .

DEIRDRE   AIMEE
Sounds good . . .   Okay, I can make a 7:05 train.

DEIRDRE

Thanks, Aimee, I'm embarrassed we had to do this—

AIMEE

Hey, first time for everything, right?

Erik hands Aimee her phone. Aimee returns to the kitchen to help.

DEIRDRE

(*to Erik*)
Are you too drunk to thank your daughter?

BRIGID

This is all from a local bakery . . .

DEIRDRE

(*more pointed*)
Hey, are you too drunk to thank your daughter?

This pisses Erik off, but he ignores Deirdre. Richard joins the table.

RICHARD

So what we've got is—this is rugelach, vanilla cupcakes, a chocolate croissant . . .

DEIRDRE

Wow . . . well today I officially fell off the Weight Watchers wagon, so . . . man, these all look good . . . I'll have, uh . . . I'll have—

ERIK

Give her the one with all the frosting, that's the one she wants.

Beat. That was the one Deirdre wanted, but now she's too stung.

DEIRDRE

I'll have, the, uh . . . I'll, uh . . . / I'm gonna . . .

RICHARD

Which one can I get you?

DEIRDRE

Just gonna / . . . [sit here for a minute] . . .

MOMO
(waking, barely audible, mumbled)
. . . nairywheres do we blag werstrus, doll sezzer / big sussten
back . . . sezz it whairidoll . . . er hairin sildern fernal garn ackening ery or loddinsezz . . .

DEIRDRE	BRIGID
. . . I'm gonna take her to the bathroom, yeah Erik? . . . / okay? . . .	You okay, Momes? . . .

BRIGID	ERIK
I can help you—	Yeah . . .

DEIRDRE

No I'm good.

ERIK
(to Richard)
Would you help her get Momo settled upstairs, / I don't want
her lifting her by herself . . .

RICHARD

Sure . . .

BRIGID

Dad, I said *I'd* help . . .

ERIK

No, stay here, will you? / Stay here . . .

Deirdre assists Momo into her wheelchair as Aimee returns from the kitchen.

BRIGID

Why?

ERIK

I wanna talk to you guys about how . . .

AIMEE

What?

ERIK

. . . we might be moving soon if, uh—

DEIRDRE

(wheeling Momo out)
There we go, Mom . . .

AIMEE

But I thought—the sewers won't be in yet . . .

Deirdre continues to roll Momo toward the basement door.

DEIRDRE	MOMO
Yeah, tell 'em about the sewers. /	*(mumbling unintelligibly until she exits)* . . . wheres'll her annear . . . do you go hole in a wheres do you go hole in a wheres do go hole in a where to go hole in a wheres . . . where do we go hole in a . . .

AIMEE	BRIGID
What's going on?	. . . Mom . . . [what's wrong?] . . .

ERIK   DEIRDRE
Nothing, nothing stay here,   *(to Brigid)*
okay?—everyone's okay . . .   I'm okay, stay here . . .
   (to Richard)
Would you let them in upstairs?

Deirdre and Momo exit.

RICHARD

Sure . . .

BRIGID   **UPSTAIRS:**
Dad. What's wrong?   *Richard goes upstairs, opens the*
                                  upstairs door and waits offstage
                                  in the hallway for Momo and
                                  Deirdre to get off the elevator.

ERIK

Nothing, everyone's okay, all right? . . .

AIMEE

Are you sick?

ERIK

No no, no one's sick, we're good, just, we sold the lake property,
okay? / To help with—

AIMEE

Okay . . .

BRIGID

What . . . when . . . ?

ERIK

[Not important] . . . St. Paul's let me go, okay, so we've had to /
tighten our belts and we're figuring out—

BRIGID

Why would they let you go?

ERIK

—that's not [important]—I'm not getting my pension now, they could fire me before it kicked in, all right / so now—

AIMEE

They can take away / your pension—?

ERIK

It's [complicated]—they're a private school so / they can do whatever—

AIMEE

But—why did they fire you?

ERIK

It's [complicated]—they have this morality code, okay?, / St. Paul's makes—

AIMEE

Okay . . .

ERIK

—you sign it / and if you—

BRIGID

Why would a morality code—were you, like, selling drugs on the playground?

ERIK

There was an incident and . . . all right?, so / they could—

BRIGID

What kind of—

ERIK

They could fire me . . . because of this incident, it's—

AIMEE

What are you talking about?

ERIK

I cheated on your mom, with, uh, a teacher from school and . . . we're okay but, I realize this is a lot to just [unload] . . . you guys okay?—

AIMEE	**BRIGID**
[Uh, not really . . .]	Just . . . [keep going] . . .

ERIK

—we worked through it, okay?, / we met with Father Quinn and . . .

AIMEE

Okay . . .

ERIK

. . . we're good, but people talk and we don't want you hearing from other people, okay? / We'd rather you hear it from us, okay? . . .

AIMEE

Okay, so . . . okay, so you guys . . . you just want us to . . . just . . . to know? . . .

ERIK

Yeah, and I'm already at a Walmart in Danville / just to keep money coming in—

AIMEE

God, Dad . . . for how long?—

BRIGID

Why the one in Danville?

ERIK

I don't want kids from school seeing me there. Something full-time should open up this spring, so . . . / the trick's been . . .

AIMEE

. . . so . . .

ERIK

. . . the cost of taking care of Momo's been a surprise, / you wouldn't even believe how much the [medical stuff costs]—

BRIGID	AIMEE
Are you guys . . .	. . . okay . . .
	So you're behind?
	How much are you behind?

	ERIK
Can Mom not retire now?—	I don't want you [worrying about]—

AIMEE

Would I be able to help out? . . . or—is it too much for me to even—

ERIK

I think—you've lost your job / and'll have your own medical stuff to [worry about]—

AIMEE

Okay, I know, I know but I still want to know how deep a hole you're in.

Being buzzed almost makes things worse for Aimee and Brigid.

UPSTAIRS:
Richard now holds the door open; Deirdre wheels Momo inside. She doesn't get far before she hears the argument downstairs; it stops her from taking Momo to the bathroom. Instead, Deirdre goes to the top of the stairs to listen. Richard instinctively goes to Momo, waits with her.

ERIK

The plan is to sell the house and rent an apartment, we don't need space / anymore . . .

BRIGID

Are there even apartments in Scranton? / Who lives in—

THE HUMANS

133

<table>
<tr><td>

AIMEE

Of course there are—
</td><td>

ERIK

Hey, getting a place on one
level will be good, Mom won't
be climbing stairs—
</td></tr>
</table>

AIMEE

It doesn't sound good, Dad / —it sounds like you're in a deep
hole—

ERIK

I'm working it out, Aimee—

AIMEE

Do you have *anything* saved? *Dad*, do you have any / savings?—

ERIK

We don't *have* savings, Aimee / *we've been stretched*—

AIMEE

—okay, okay *well you're telling us this when you're drunk* / so
sorry if I'm getting frustrated . . .

ERIK

—well we haven't had savings for years.

BRIGID

Have you asked Uncle John to help?

AIMEE

He lives in a trailer, / you think—

BRIGID

That doesn't mean he has no money—

AIMEE

That's *exactly* what it means, / grow up . . . [fucking baby] . . .

<table>
<tr><td>

BRIGID

Relax, I'm just . . . [I'm
shocked, I don't know what
</td><td>

ERIK

Don't get upset with her, hey
this is on me—
</td></tr>
</table>

BRIGID

I'm saying . . .] sorry I'm not
grown up like you and make
a ton of money—

AIMEE

Right, you've got no choice but to collect unemployment / while
you try to—it's not unfair for you to get some marketable skills—

BRIGID   ERIK
That's not fair—I can't get a   Hey easy, cut it out. Stop it,
break if I'm working   both of you, stop, this is on me
full-time . . .   and—
                                        (recognizing Brigid's distress)
                                     —hey, I'm working it out, /
                                     I love your mom, we're good . . .

*Brigid isn't sure what to do; something's fallen apart for her,
thoughts spinning . . .*

UPSTAIRS:
Deirdre has decided to go downstairs; she begins her descent.

BRIGID

No, I'm glad you're working it out but—
you're *good* but you're not sleeping and Mom's still eating her
feelings, / it's freaking me out—

AIMEE

(referring to Deirdre at the top of the stairs)
Brigid.

*Brigid turns, sees Deirdre at the top of the staircase. She heads
upstairs to apologize.*

BRIGID

Mom . . . / I didn't mean it . . .

ERIK

Stay here . . .

Aimee goes after Brigid.

ERIK
Would you stay down here, please? Brigid!

AIMEE	**DEIRDRE**
Dad give her some space, okay, we're doing our best—	Go talk to your father, please, / I *know* you think something's wrong with me, it's not a news flash.

BRIGID
Mom—I will, but—I don't [think that]—I think something's wrong with *everyone*—please don't act like a martyr / when I'm trying to apologize . . . you think *I'm* wrong to not wanna get married in a church so—

AIMEE	**MOMO**
Hey, hey, you're sorry, don't yell at her, okay / . . . just chill out?	*(barely audible)* Nevery blacken where you come back do we go do we wheren blezzick . . . blacken where you come back do we go do . . .

ERIK
Can you guys come down and talk to me please!

THUD.

BRIGID
(to Richard)
Can you go up and tell that lady how loud she's being?

ERIK	**RICHARD**
Brigid!	I will, just relax.

THUD.

AIMEE
Dad, / please shuttup . . .

BRIGID	MOMO
I'll do it myself . . . / I need a breather—	*(mumbled)* Nevery blacken where you come back do we go do we wheren blezzick . . .

Momo's growing agitation captures Aimee's attention.
Deirdre is massaging Momo's hand, for herself as much as for Momo.

RICHARD	AIMEE
Hey, hey hey no, no—let's go for a walk, okay?—	*(regarding Momo, to Deirdre)* . . . is she okay?

ERIK

Brigid, please come talk to me.

BRIGID

(to Erik)
I'm gonna ask that woman to stop banging her fucking feet.

Brigid exits. This is worse than if she yelled at Erik.
Richard stops Erik from following her.

RICHARD	MOMO
Hey, let me . . .	. . . nevery where do we go back do we never go hole you bitch / . . . nevery hole backenser he did thisserwe go black, go black . . .

Deirdre walks to the staircase.

DEIRDRE

I've gotta . . . [go get some water downstairs] . . . I can't hear her now . . .

ERIK	MOMO
Yeah, I got this . . . *(to Aimee)* Go with her? She's okay, just	. . . nevery where do we go back do we never go hole you bitch . . . nevery black hole you

ERIK	MOMO
give us some room . . . . . . go with Mom, okay? *Go with Mom.*	do we you did this do we back . . . *(fixed on Erik)* Go hole. Go hole! Go hole! / Ohhhhhh God they're every- where! They're coming to you you bitch what's wrong with you . . .

Aimee has never seen Momo like this. Aimee heads downstairs to look after Deirdre.
Erik tends to Momo.

DEIRDRE	ERIK
(descending the stairs, barely intelligible) . . . what's wrong with me . . .	Hey, hey . . . shhh . . . shhhh . . .

Momo is having her first real fit of the day. It's pretty terrifying. Erik has seen it before, but it's still hard for him. It's like she's possessed.

MOMO	ERIK
. . . Go home to fuck you *you bitch!* . . . Aaaaawwwwhhhh . . . where do you go hole! They're coming to *what's wrong with you* did this . . . aaaawwwwhhhh . . . where do go hole in a wheres . . . *(tapering to barely audible)* . . . where do go hole in a wheres do go hole in a wheres do go hole in a where to go hole in a wheres . . .	Okay, okay, okay . . . we'll go for a walk . . . okay . . . shhhh . . . . . . shhhhhh . . . you're okay . . . shhhhhh . . . shhhhhh . . . you're okay . . . shhhhhh . . . there we go, there we go, shhhhh . . . shhhhh . . . that's good, you're okay . . . shhhhh . . .

UPSTAIRS:

Erik wheels Momo around like she's a baby, calming her. Her screams subside. During the following scene, Erik stays with her, maybe massaging/holding her hand . . . Is he comforting her or is she giving him *comfort?*

DOWNSTAIRS:

Deirdre sits on the couch, takes a glass of water from Aimee. Long beat.

DEIRDRE

If I ever get like that . . . I don't ever want you guys to have to . . .

Beat.

AIMEE

Mom . . . I'm sorry.

Beat.

DEIRDRE

I'm sorry you're sick.

Beat.

DEIRDRE
(this has been on her mind . . .)
That e-mail about us being electrons wasn't *religious*—it was from a *science* website . . .
(beat)
. . . I drank too much. I gotta use the [bathroom] . . .

Deirdre starts up the staircase.

AIMEE

Mom—sorry, it smells really bad in there.

DEIRDRE
(not looking back, half to herself)
Shoulda got Brigid that candle.

UPSTAIRS:
Deirdre passes Erik and Momo on her way to the bathroom.

ERIK

Hey, sorry this was . . . [a total fucking nightmare] . . .

Erik goes to embrace Deirdre.

ERIK	DEIRDRE
I love you.	No, no, no . . . I don't feel good. Lemme get her to the bathroom before we go . . . c'mon, Mom . . . there you go . . .

Deirdre helps Momo into the bathroom as Aimee ascends the stairs and proceeds to put on her coat.

AIMEE

I'm gonna go for a walk around the block . . .

ERIK

Are you okay? Hey are you—

AIMEE

Yeah, I want some air, Dad.

Erik nods. Aimee ignores him as she puts on her coat.
Erik searches for something to bridge the gap, to stop her from going.

ERIK

I've been losing sleep trying to—I was saying to Father Quinn in how . . . / just *thinking* about losing you guys gets me thinking about . . .

AIMEE

What're you [saying?] . . .

ERIK

. . . when you were gone, when—

AIMEE

What're you [saying?] . . .

ERIK

—this fireman was holding a body with your same suit on? . . .

Dad . . .

ERIK

. . . but with a coat of ash melted onto her?, like she got turned into a statue like . . .

AIMEE

Dad . . .

Aimee aches for her father and wants to stay, but she needs to take care of herself.

ERIK

. . . there was gray in her eyes and mouth even, it was . . . like her whole . . .
    (a discovery)
[. . . face was gone . . .]

Aimee has already moved to leave, she isn't registering Erik's thoughts.

AIMEE

The car company will call when they're ready, leave your phone by the window so it'll ring.

Aimee exits.

Erik is alone for a few beats, lost, processing his discovery.

Toilet flush brings him back to reality.
He takes out his phone per Aimee's instructions and places it on the windowsill when—

He notices a shadow move in the alley—what was it?

He gets the LED lantern from the other room and walks back to the window to get a better look, but it's so dark outside, the glass mostly reflects his image. He stares for a few beats.

DOWNSTAIRS:

A few pots and pans hanging on the edge of the drying rack (just visible in the kitchen alley) fall and CRASH to the floor.

ERIK

(calling down)
Brigid . . . ?

No answer. Erik descends the spiral staircase . . .

DOWNSTAIRS: **UPSTAIRS:**

Erik arrives downstairs, where it's brighter.
Erik turns the lantern off, places it on the counter.
He begins to pick up the pots and pans . . .

Deirdre and Momo exit the bathroom.

The main upstairs door opens revealing Aimee.
She holds the door open, allowing light to spill into the upstairs rooms.

AIMEE

Guys, the car's out front . . .

DEIRDRE

All right, get her coat, will you? . . .

AIMEE

(looking for Erik)
Is Dad . . . ?

DEIRDRE

[I dunno.]

(calling down)
. . . Dad!

ERIK

(calling up)
I heard you . . .

Aimee helps Deirdre get Momo into her coat and back into the wheelchair.

DEIRDRE

Where's Brigid?

AIMEE

With Rich . . .

Deirdre looks to Aimee for more information as Aimee helps Momo into her coat.

AIMEE

. . . she's embarrassed, she's . . . [I don't even wanna get into it.]
(calling down)
. . . Dad! . . .

ERIK

(calling up)
Yeah, coming . . .

Aimee wheels Momo out of the apartment, exiting with Momo's barely discernable mumbling trailing . . .

Deirdre goes to exit, but stops, remembering something.

DEIRDRE

(to Erik, calling down)
Hey, can you grab Mom's blanket and the pan we brought?

ERIK

Uh-huh.

DOWNSTAIRS:	UPSTAIRS:
Erik goes back to picking up the pots and pans that fell.	*Deirdre, alone upstairs.*
	She takes one last look around, gets an idea: she quietly removes the Virgin Mary statue from her purse and places it in the windowsill. She exits.

Having cleaned up the pots and pans, Erik searches for the specific pan they brought; finding it, he exits the kitchen and places the pan on the table.

Erik searches for the blanket. He finds the blanket near the couch. He folds it.

All of the downstairs lights flicker out.

Complete darkness.

ERIK

Shit.

Erik puts the blanket down; he searches for the lantern on the counter, bumping chairs at the table as he stumbles past . . . then—

UPSTAIRS:	DOWNSTAIRS:
In complete darkness, the phone vibrates and lights up in the upstairs windowsill; the phone vibrates.	

vibrates.

vibrates.

UPSTAIRS:	**DOWNSTAIRS:**
vibrates.	*—Erik finally finds the lantern, turns it on. The LED lantern in hand, he flips all the fuse box switches to no avail.*
vibrates.	
vibrates.	

ERIK

[Was that the phone?]

Then stops. Then—

vibrates.

> *He flips the fuse box switches again, then—the LED lantern in hand—goes up the staircase to answer the phone.*

vibrates.

vibrates.

vibrates.

vibrates.

Erik arrives at the windowsill, picks up the phone.

ERIK

Hello? . . . hello—

The RUMBLE of the trash compactor strikes up again outside the basement door. In the darkness, it sounds louder than before, more disturbing.

. . . he pockets his phone, follows the noise back downstairs.

The RUMBLE continues.

Erik heads down the hallway toward the origin of the noise— pushes through his anxiety, opens the basement door; fluorescent light from the hallway spills in— the RUMBLE of the trash compactor is now even louder but more familiar, more like a loud trash compactor.

The trash compactor completes its cycle.

Silence.

Erik comes back inside but the spring-hinged door doesn't stay open, plunging the place into darkness as it closes.
Erik goes to get a chair to prop it open when—

A THUD from above the staircase startles him, he drops the lantern . . .

Sounds of Erik's heavy breathing,
Erik groping for a chair,
Erik dragging it to the main downstairs door . . .

Suddenly fluorescent hallway light spills into the space via the basement door. Erik is propping it open with a chair.
The downstairs is now much brighter.

He picks up the dropped lantern from the floor, which has remained on, holds it up toward the direction of the stairs . . .

Then, from the depths of the basement hallway, a new sound.

. . . click-clack, click-clack, click-clack . . .
Erik backs away from the hallway entrance.
. . . click-clack, click-clack, click-clack . . .
Erik's breath shortens.
. . . click-CLACK, click-CLACK, click-CLACK . . .
Erik's heart pounds, he looks toward the door.
. . . click-CLACK, click-CLACK, click-CLACK . . .

In a breath, an elderly Chinese woman passes the basement door on her way down the hall, wheeling her laundry in a cheap metal cart with a busted wheel.
The sounds slowly disappear as she rolls the cart down the hall.
. . . click-clack, click-clack, click-clack . . .
. . . click-clack, click-clack, click-clack . . .

This perfectly ordinary event leaves Erik feeling overwhelmed; it triggers a few ugly sobs.
Erik's face is visible via the light of the lantern.

He is quietly terrified, mumbling the Hail Mary.
Is he recovering from a panic attack?

ERIK

[What's happening to me? . . . What's wrong with me? This cannot be happening to me . . . oh God, how could I have gotten that worked up?]

DOWNSTAIRS:
Erik can't quite move yet;
he clutches a support beam or sits in a chair, taking steady breaths, trying to recover.

Alone, Erik collects himself, still unsure of what just transpired.
He goes into the kitchen and splashes some water on his face.
He can't quite believe it. He can't quite grasp it.
Rattled, the event's released something for him—a strange weight's been lifted off his chest.
He takes deep breaths, trying to ground himself.
This should all last at least fifteen seconds.

UPSTAIRS:
Brigid enters.

BRIGID

(calling down)
Dad . . . the driver's gonna have to keep circling the block. Dad . . . ?

ERIK

Yeah, no here I come . . .

UPSTAIRS:	DOWNSTAIRS:
Brigid searches for something more to say.	
She goes to leave.	*Erik finds the pan.*
She stops in the doorway.	
Beat.	

UPSTAIRS:	DOWNSTAIRS:

He goes to get the blanket . . .

She comes back in again, still
searching for something to say.

BRIGID

(calling down)
It's a van for some reason, so . . . I can ride with you guys to
Penn Station . . . I'll get out with Aimee there, take the subway
back . . . it's not far . . .

ERIK

Thanks.

UPSTAIRS:
Brigid exits.

DOWNSTAIRS:
Erik is still recovering . . .
He picks up Momo's blanket.
Arms full, he realizes he's left the LED lantern lit on the table.

He puts his belongings down; turns the lantern off, darkening
the basement.
This greatly sharpens the shaft of fluorescent hallway light pour-
ing through the propped-open door.

It has a tunnel-like quality.

Erik picks up his belongings again, turns toward the door and
notices the shaft of light.

He steps into it.
He considers it for a moment.
He takes a deep breath.
He walks toward the door.

With no remaining natural or electric light,
the apartment's architecture seems to have vanished . . .
. . . even the indirect moonlight from the upstairs window is gone . . .
. . . the only defined shape comes from the lighted doorway.

STEPHEN KARAM

Erik exits into the hallway and out of sight.

A very long beat.

The propped-open door begins to slowly close entirely on its own; the weight of the chair can no longer hold it open.

The door clicks shut, rendering the space a deep, true black.

THE END

STEPHEN KARAM is the author of *Sons of the Prophet*, a finalist for the 2012 Pulitzer Prize and winner of the 2012 Drama Critics Circle, Outer Critics Circle, Lucille Lortel and Hull-Warriner awards for Best Play. Other plays include *Speech & Debate*, the inaugural production of Roundabout Underground; *columbinus* (New York Theatre Workshop) and *Dark Sisters*, an original chamber opera with composer Nico Muhly. He has written the screenplay for a film adaptation of Chekhov's *The Seagull* (starring Annette Bening) and a new adaptation of *The Cherry Orchard*, which will premiere on Broadway in 2016. He is the recipient of the inaugural Sam Norkin Off-Broadway Drama Desk Award. Stephen grew up in Scranton, PA, and is a graduate of Brown University.